SMALL BUSINESS IN THE CLINTON YEARS

*A Comprehensive Guide to Critical Issues from
the National Federation of Independent Business,
the Nation's Leading Small Business Advocacy Organization.*

SMALL BUSINESS IN
What Your Company Must D

THE CLINTON YEARS
to Survive and Succeed

EDITED BY S. JACKSON FARIS,
President & Chief Executive Officer
National Federation of Independent Business
Washington, D.C.

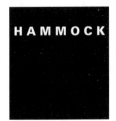

HAMMOCK publishing inc.

NASHVILLE

Copyright ©1993 National Federation of Independent Business

All rights reserved. No part of this book may be reproduced or transmitted in any form or by any means, electronic or mechanical, including photocopying, recording or by any information storage and retrieval system, without permission in writing from NFIB and the publisher.

National Federation of Independent Business
600 Maryland Ave. S.W.
Suite 700
Washington, D.C. 20024
(202) 554-9000

To order additional copies, call:
1-800-345-8112

For quantity sales information, contact:
Hammock Publishing Inc.
3322 West End Avenue, Suite 700
Nashville, TN 37203
(615) 385-9745

ISBN: 0-9635489-0-5

10 9 8 7 6 5 4 3 2 1

Manufactured in the United States of America

Acknowledgements

This book could not have been produced in such a short period of time were it not for the decades of experience and knowledge of NFIB's Washington, D.C. staff. Special thanks to: John Motley, Wendy Lechner, Kelleen Jackson, Mary Reed, Harriet James, Leslie Aubin, D.J. Gribbin and Lori Robertson. Thanks also to David Cullen, Denny Dennis, Kate Vislay, Pat Lawry and Kenneth Furlough. Also, Pam Camplin in Nashville and Bob Wimberley in Little Rock, Ark. And to the nearly 1,000 other employees of NFIB.

Thanks also to the editorial staff of Hammock Publishing: Julia Evers, Rex Hammock, Adele Rowan and Bobby Stark; along with Bill Hudgins. Thanks also to: Michael Nott, Roger Clayton, Melanie Brogli and Jack Pentzer.

This book is dedicated to the
nation's small business owners,
America's most endangered species.

Contents

Editor's Note
xv

Introduction
SMALL BUSINESS AND
JOBS, JOBS, JOBS
1

Chapter 1
THE ROLE OF SMALL BUSINESS
IN AMERICA'S ECONOMY:
"MOST AMERICANS DON'T KNOW THIS"
11

Chapter 2
PRESIDENT BILL CLINTON:
A FRIEND OF SMALL BUSINESS, OR FOE?
17

Chapter 3
SMALL BUSINESS ISSUES
FACING A NEW PRESIDENT
27

Chapter 4
HEALTH CARE:
HEALING A SICK SYSTEM
33

Chapter 5
TAXES
61

Chapter 6
THE BUDGET DEFICIT
73

Chapter 7
THE CLINTON PLAN TO ENCOURAGE
SMALL BUSINESS CREATION AND GROWTH
AND A FEW MORE IDEAS
77

Chapter 8
LABOR AND THE WORK PLACE
83

Chapter 9
REDUCING THE CRUSHING WEIGHT OF
GOVERNMENT REGULATION AND PAPERWORK
107

Chapter 10
PROTECTING THE ENVIRONMENT,
PROTECTING SMALL BUSINESS
123

Chapter 11
WHAT SMALL BUSINESS OWNERS MUST DO
135

Chapter 12
SMALL BUSINESS SURVIVAL GUIDE
147

OPINIONS OF SMALL BUSINESS OWNERS ON
KEY ISSUES FACING THE CLINTON
ADMINISTRATION AND THE 103RD CONGRESS
161

CONGRESSIONAL DIRECTORY
173

Editor's Note

This book is a comprehensive examination of some of the challenging small business issues the president and Congress will be addressing, most likely during his first three years in office. Yet, while the issues are complex, we have attempted to keep this book free from the Washington-speak and bureaucratic lingo that, at times, seem to add to the complexity of any issue. We apologize when we fail to keep it simple.

Small Business in the Clinton Years was written and went to press during those frenzied days between election and inauguration. Indeed some may be reading this in the days and weeks prior to January 20, 1993. Our primary purpose was to provide a quick yet thorough guide to critical public policy issues which will directly affect small business owners during the Clinton administration. Events will surely date some of the specifics of its contents, but most of the material will be relevant when the "First 100 Days" are distant memories.

This book is written for the owners of small business, but we believe the friends of small business "inside the Beltway" will find it to be a helpful reference for the coming battles.

Introduction

Small Business and Jobs, Jobs, Jobs

In the days immediately leading up to and following the election of Bill Clinton as the 42nd President of the United States of America, the Washington office of NFIB, the National Federation of Independent Business, received concerned calls from many of the 600,000 small business owners who are its members.

"What will the election of Bill Clinton mean for my business?"

The refrain seemed almost universal among the owners of small businesses around the country — even from the many who actively supported and campaigned for the new president. Why? Because change, any change, gives small business owners cause for concern. For reflection. For analysis. For planning. For adaptation. For renewed determination to succeed.

This book is one response by NFIB to the chorus of requests for information on how small businesses may be affected by policy issues likely to emerge during a Clinton administration, and how business owners should prepare for them. In this book, we examine small business-related issues on which he campaigned. Issues with which he was involved as governor of Arkansas. Issues that are a part of the agenda of those who formed the coalition which supported his impressive, successful campaign.

But you don't have to read the entire book to hear the most reassuring response I can offer a small business owner concerned with what the new president means for his or her business. It is as simple as this: The success of President Bill Clinton is linked directly to the success of small business during his first term in office. Period.

It will be years before historians and economists verify this statement, but the facts available today support the following prediction: If the policies and approach of a Clinton administration establish an environment in which small businesses can be created and thrive, then President Clinton will successfully address what he described as his top three priorities: jobs, jobs, jobs.

The economic history of our nation clearly teaches one fundamental lesson above all others: Allow small businesses to soar, and they will create jobs, jobs, jobs.

However, if an adversarial environment is created in which owners and potential owners of small businesses are burdened with an even heavier yoke of governmental regulation, punitive tax policy and mandated programs, procedures and employee benefits, then small business — the major source of real job growth in today's economy — will no longer have the ability to fuel a sustained economic recovery. And the American electorate has proven, currently with the new president as the beneficiary, its unwill-

Introduction

ingness to support those at the helm during a sluggish economy.

Come next election, "if 70 percent of the people still think the country is on the wrong (economic) track, we're dead," one Clinton aide told a *Wall Street Journal* reporter two weeks after the election.

The Arkansas Model

Another reassuring point for small business owners: As governor of Arkansas, Bill Clinton on many occasions supported, on occasion even conceived, measures that created a positive environment for small business, an impressive record we examine in Chapter 2. Indeed, he was the first U.S. governor to receive the coveted "Guardian of Small Business Award" from NFIB. Also, a testament to his record is the support he received from many small business owners in Arkansas, those who know him best.

If he continues in this tradition, President Clinton will find small business owners responding by expanding their businesses and creating new and better jobs.

However, many small business owners worry that President Clinton with one hand will make "jobs, jobs, jobs" his top priority, but with his other, will work to enact programs outlined in his campaign that will burden these same business people with the task of solving some of the nation's most complex social and political problems.

President Clinton will find small business owners ready

to support him when the issue is the creation of jobs; ready to fight when the issue results in more government mandates, higher taxes, or employer-based solutions to social problems.

Jobs, Jobs, Jobs

On Election Day 1993, according to polls conducted for the television networks by Voter Research Surveys, 43 percent of voters cited "economy/jobs" as the issue determining their vote. That's twice the response given any single issue, including the budget deficit, health care, abortion, education, the environment, taxes, foreign policy or family values.

If the creation of jobs is the single most important issue to those who elected Bill Clinton, then government policies affecting small businesses should be the most critical concerns facing the new president. For President Clinton knows the one truth on which nearly all economists agree: In America today, the overwhelming majority of new jobs are created by small, independent businesses. According to a November 1992 report by the Congressional Joint Economic Committee, small businesses created 67 percent of the net new jobs from 1982-1990, while the smallest of these firms — those with less than 20 employees — are credited with generating 51 percent of the increased employment.

For the past decade, while large corporations have laid off workers as the result of recession, mergers and efforts

Introduction

to improve productivity, it has been small business owners who have added to the work force.

There is no reason to believe this trend will not continue. That is, unless federal, state and local governments take away the incentive for entrepreneurs to start and grow businesses. Of course, no politician would ever openly or even willfully desire to punish the small business owner. However, in their desire to fix all of society's problems and to respond to caring citizens who have genuine concerns for these critical issues, elected politicians repeatedly enact laws with lofty goals. Unfortunately, the resulting rules, regulations and mandated benefits and policies, when implemented, can crush the small business person with paperwork, regulatory constraints, petty bureaucratic hassles and wasteful costs that do nothing to solve the targeted problem.

The mandate of the American electorate was to create jobs. Job creation takes precedence over all other worthwhile and critical issues. Yet the owners of small businesses, those who in reality are the individuals with the most power to create new jobs (except government make-work programs), fear their investment will be rewarded with additional regulatory burdens and increased taxes. Such levies take the form of payroll taxes and taxes on profits as well as the hidden taxes of higher interest rates, inflation and administrative costs.

Small business owners, like all patriotic Americans, want to see their new president succeed. They will support him until he throws the weight of the presidency behind the issues that threaten their ability to survive and succeed.

What Do Small Business Owners Want?

Therefore, this book is about issues, not personalities or political parties. During its 50-year history (President Clinton's inaugural year corresponds with our golden anniversary) NFIB has worked with presidents from both parties in presenting the concerns and beliefs of independent business owners. With more than 600,000 members, NFIB is far and away the largest, oldest and most effective small business advocacy group in America. For instance, it is one of the few national associations of any type that has governmental relations offices in Washington, D.C., *and* all 50 state capitals. In a survey of Capitol Hill staffers, *Fortune* magazine named NFIB one of the "ten toughest lobbies" in Washington.

Just how important are the views of small business owners? Consider that more than 99 percent of all businesses in America are small and independent.

Small business owners work in every industry and trade. They are male and female and of every ethnic background and religious belief. They belong to every imaginable political party, or refuse adamantly to join any. On issues not directly tied to their ability to succeed in a free enterprise system, their opinions scatter to the four winds.

So what will the views of small business owners likely be during the Clinton administration?

Introduction

Despite their diversity, here are a few bedrock concerns and beliefs shared almost universally by the men and women who own and run the nation's small businesses:

•*Small business owners believe the government that governs least, governs best. They resent the way elected officials — the same men and women who have allowed the government to spend absurdly beyond its means — are constantly enacting laws that result in reams of regulations and mandates dictating how a small business must be run.*

•*For this reason, small business owners almost universally agree that government — federal, state and local — should tax less and spend less. They are strong believers that the men and women who are elected to govern need to have the discipline to run a government that lives within its means.*

•*The supremacy of private property rights is nearly universally supported by small business owners. Small business owners are extremely patriotic, loyal citizens who are the first to support the common good, but they have worked hard to create and build what they have and are committed to passing it on to their children. Therefore, they greatly oppose measures by any level of government — even well-meaning measures — which result in the confiscation or devaluation of an individual's private property without equitable compensation.*

> *Perhaps the strongest thread of belief running through the hearts and souls of small business owners is a belief in the individual. They are kindred minds with the small business owners like John Hancock and Benjamin Franklin who in July 1776 risked their lives, their fortunes and their sacred honors by signing the Declaration of Independence. Today, the vast majority of small businesses are created not by individuals expecting to start the next Apple Computer, but by committed individuals dedicated to the American tradition of individual freedom and the right to determine one's own destiny.*

Small businesses today are run by men and women with a deeply felt commitment to the cause of freedom and free enterprise. Their desire to run a business is a tradition seemingly etched in the nation's genetic code. This tradition and inclination toward entrepreneurship is almost unique in the world. Indeed, this small business spirit is a beacon so bright, even today it attracts like swarming moths determined young entrepreneurs from all around the world.

By their nature, American entrepreneurs and the people who work for them, are optimists. They would not have risked their savings, in many instances their homes, their names and their futures, on starting and running a small business unless they had faith in a system that allows them to seek the opportunity they believe to be within

Introduction

their grasp. Take away that faith and you destroy the passion that propels these pioneer-spirited individuals. Try to solve all society's problems by loading them on their backs and the only result will be broken backs.

Protecting An Endangered Species: Small Business

As president and chief executive officer of NFIB, it is my great fortune to daily visit with small business owners throughout America. Not only do we meet in official settings and formal gatherings, but I get to see them in their stores, factories, offices, garages, restaurants, even their cars and homes in which more and more independent business owners are basing their operations.

For 50 years, NFIB has represented such men and women in Washington and in all the state capitals.

Unfortunately, during those 50 years, our fight has become increasingly difficult as higher and higher barriers are placed in the way of struggling entrepreneurs. At times it seems that our elected officials and the vast bureaucracies they have created are conspiring to wipe out the species of small business owner.

So we return to the concern of small business owners and the priorities of President Clinton and find the two tied together in a vital partnership.

To grow, to flourish, to succeed, to survive, small business and President Clinton depend upon each other.

S. Jackson Faris
November 30, 1992

1

The Role of Small Business in America's Economy: "Most Americans Don't Know This"

On his first visit to the nation's capital after the election, President Clinton (then president-elect) followed a White House meeting with former President Bush with a tour of small businesses along Washington's Georgia Avenue. "In the last 12 years, 85 percent of all new jobs in America have been created in groups of under 50," Clinton told reporters, adding, "Most Americans don't know this."

He's right.

There was a time in America when destiny appeared to award the future to big business. It seemed a universally accepted belief that bigger was always better.

"What's good for the country is good for General Motors, and what's good for General Motors is good for the country," Charles Erwin Wilson told the Senate Armed Services Committee in 1952.

The "little guys" running the small businesses in America's hometowns were viewed as quaint little lap dogs, out of place among the forecasts of a "new industrial state."

Today, just listen.

That's not the roar of lap dogs, no, listen closer, those are bulldogs. They are the small business bulldogs who employ the majority of American workers and who, for the past decade, have produced the vast majority of all new jobs.

As President Clinton pointed out on his small business stroll, the role these businesses play in the American economy today is still overlooked by many.

You know them. They are on every street corner: restaurants, dry cleaners, plumbing contractors, gas stations, florists, manufacturers, drug stores, grocery stores, farms, repair shops and hair stylists.

They're not owned by rich fat cats. Not by any stretch of the imagination. Typically, the owners of these firms employ about five workers with whom they toil, shoulder-to-shoulder. They take from the business an average of $40,000 per year in salary and profit. As much of the profits as possible are immediately plowed back into the company, often just to keep it afloat.

More than 5 million small enterprises dot the American landscape. These small businesses employ some 59 million people. In addition, self-employment is the livelihood of more than 11 million Americans.

Today, business ownership remains the American dream. Indeed, it has become the model for dreams throughout the world.

The Role of Small Business in the Economy

Small business owners are women and men, all races and ethnic origins, every age range, every nationality, every economic background, from large cities and small towns, inner city and rural. The common thread is independence and a devotion to free enterprise. With this thread, they have woven the strong fabric of the American economy.

Small businesses are represented in all industries, but together, they are the world class creator of a single item: jobs. More than 57 percent of the nation's private work force is employed in small firms. And given an environment free from burdensome governmental interference, small businesses have shown they can boost the economy with millions more jobs.

And small business has historically helped the economy in other ways, among them: technological innovation.

Thanks to the entrepreneurship of small business, we have such life staples as personal computers, air travel, insulin, xerography, air conditioning, lasers, pacemakers and many more. Studies have shown that while small business and independent inventors are responsible for about half the important innovations this century, they also produced them using fewer financial resources and fewer people and brought them to market more rapidly.

One study conducted for the Small Business Administration by Gellman Research Associates found that small firms produced more than twice the innovations per employee than did large firms and brought them to market in two-thirds the amount of time. Furthermore, they usually did so without the benefits (or liabilities) of government financial support.

But it is not just what they do that makes small businesses succeed, it's how they do it. Aside from technological innovations, small businesses have led the way in reforming the processes of production. A few obvious examples are Henry Ford, Ray Kroc and Sam Walton.

While owners of small businesses may admire the success of Ray Kroc and Sam Walton, very few of them expect to grow their eateries or stores into retail giants like McDonald's or Wal-Mart.

They just want the right to run their businesses their own way and to achieve their own level of success within the freedom of the market economy. They adamantly oppose the government — which can't even get its own finances in order — telling them how to operate their businesses.

And, contrary to what many legislators and regulators apparently believe, small business owners do not want to trample on the rights of the work force. They live and die by the work force. They simply want the freedom to tailor their wages and benefits to the individual nuances of the labor market in which they operate – the freedom to add jobs. They don't want lawmakers – who don't have to abide by their own labor laws – pushing onto them a one-size-fits-all mandated plan that only serves to raise the cost of hiring new workers.

And they don't want to be burdened under more costs imposed by a Congress trying to solve social problems

The Role of Small Business in the Economy

with more federal mandates.

In 1840, the French historian and author of *Democracy in America*, Alexis de Tocqueville, provided one of the more interesting observations ever made about the American economy. He wrote: " ... what most astonished me in the United States is not so much the marvelous grandeur of some undertakings as the innumerable multitude of small ones."

On his first day in Washington as President-elect, President Clinton reminded the American people about something still astonishing: the economic roar of the nation's multitude of small businesses.

President Clinton and the 103rd Congress have in their unique power the ability to keep the roar alive.

Most Americans don't know this.

2

President Bill Clinton: A Friend of Small Business, or Foe?

"Will President Clinton be a friend of small business?" Although it is being asked by small business owners across the nation, it seems at first a strange question to raise about a person who has spent his entire adult life in public office. It should be clear from his record whether or not he will support policies friendly to small businesses. (And as will be discussed, much in his record as governor of Arkansas suggests he will.)

However, in this case, the question is extremely appropriate.

Change, especially the dramatic change that comes with the election of a new president, is unsettling. Also, given the performance of some elected officials in the past, the question is justified. It seems after elections, what is said during a campaign is very different from how the official governs or legislates.

Indeed, on the campaign trail, all politicians claim to be a friend of small business and economic growth. But once elected, many attempt to solve social and political problems on the backs of those small business "friends."

In the case of President Clinton, this natural uncertainty about *any* politician is compounded by the concern he raised among small business owners with his statements on some key issues during the campaign. The issues he supported as a candidate that worry small business owners include: "striker replacement" legislation; mandated employer-sponsored health care; mandated family leave; removing caps on damages in employment discrimination suits; and repeal of a federal provision allowing states to have right-to-work laws. (Each of these issues is discussed at length in later chapters.)

These positions, which may have been adopted to gain the favor of organized labor, are nonetheless out of synch with his record as governor.

Therefore, small business owners are hoping they can get a sense of President Clinton's future by looking to Governor Clinton's past.

**Gov. Bill Clinton of Arkansas:
Friend of Small Business**

President Clinton's most recent decade-long record as governor of Arkansas is quite clear: He was a friend of that state's small businesses. In fact, he was the first governor in the nation to receive NFIB's coveted "Guardian of Small Business" award for his role in the protection of

Bill Clinton: Friend of Small Business?

small business. He respected the state's right-to-work laws and benefited from them. As the state's number one business recruiter, Clinton personally worked with businesses to keep jobs from leaving the state and to attract new employers to Arkansas. And, in so doing, the governor used the state's right-to-work status as a key selling point.

His policies helped Arkansas lead the nation in new job growth, while keeping taxing and spending in line with the growth of personal income.

Governor Bill Clinton took on controversial issues related to small business and worked hard to build consensus on complicated legislation, giving small business a central role in the policy making process. For instance, in 1986, he called a special session of the Arkansas Legislature to find a solution to rising workers' compensation costs. The resulting legislation helped to improve the system as well as control its costs.

In other areas, he consistently took positions defending small business: in preserving retail merchants' two-percent sales tax allowance, in supporting capital gains tax reduction and in seeking regulatory relief.

However, Gov. Clinton's most noted alliances with small business were his innovative solutions to help control health care costs and to improve small businesses' access to capital.

These areas are so central to small business throughout America they deserve discussion in more detail:

Controlling Health Care Costs

As governor, Clinton recognized the burden rising health care costs and group medical insurance are putting on small business. To address the problem, he commissioned legislative studies to seek ways to contain premium costs. He found that the extensive coverages mandated by state law were effectively pricing small businesses out of the group medical insurance market. The available policies were loaded down like a Christmas tree with state mandated add-on benefits. As a result, between 250,000 and 500,000 Arkansans were without health insurance.

In a 1990 meeting, Clinton alerted small business owners to a new medical insurance policy that had been approved in Ohio. By stripping out some of the traditional state mandated coverages, this no-frills policy brought premiums down. Working with small business owners, Clinton pushed for changes in regulations governing health insurance coverage and led the fight for an insurance bill that allowed insurance companies to issue limited-coverage policies at lower costs.

In early 1991, the governor signed into law the Minimum Basic Insurance Program. Commonly known as "Barebones" insurance, the policy, which recently became available, will pay for 15 days of hospital care, and a basic level of primary and preventative care, with an annual benefit limit of not less than $100,000 and a lifetime benefit of not less than $250,000. By bringing costs down, the program will help more small businesses offer basic health insurance to their employees. The Arkansas program, it should be noted, contains no mandates that employers *must* pay for employee health insurance. Yet by working with small businesses the governor helped enact a program that will allow more of them to afford employee health insurance.

Improving Access to Capital

As governor, President Clinton knew the troubles small businesses were facing when capital needed for ongoing operations or expansion was unavailable. In Arkansas, the problem was made more difficult by the state's antiquated usury (interest rate) laws governing bank lending. To address the problem, in 1982 and 1990, he endorsed controversial constitutional amendments that would change these laws, despite being up for re-election both times.

While those efforts met with limited success, Gov. Clinton looked for ways to go around the banking laws to make capital more available to small businesses. The result was the creation of the "linked deposit program" and the Arkansas Development Finance Authority.

Small business leaders, in one of their regular meetings with the governor, told him about policies in other states which allowed surplus state funds to be set aside for lower-interest small business loans. In 1991, Gov. Clinton helped create what is now the Linked Deposit Small Business Loan program, which allows up to $50 million of state funds in lending institutions to be loaned to small businesses at below market rates.

The program's objective is to make funds available to small businesses so they may survive and expand.

The program was created specifically and exclusively for small businesses. For example, a company getting a loan under the program must have no more than 75 employees or annual revenues exceeding $5 million. Also, the program is closely tied to the creation of jobs. For each $50,000 borrowed, the small business must show that it will save or create one job. (This requirement is waived for farmers.)

Another example of his support of programs that expanded access to capital is the creation of the Southern Development Bancorporation (SDB). As a means to increase loans to small businesses, in 1988 the state helped to create SDB. The corporation now has five divisions, including a traditional commercial bank, a Small Business Investment Corporation (SBIC), a micro-loan program for loans under $10,000, a real estate development division and a technical assistance division which works with small businesses to help them plan and obtain their finances. The corporation makes millions of dollars worth of SBA-guaranteed loans that would not be granted by other institutions.

Observers point to the creation of the Arkansas Development Finance Authority (ADFA) as one of the president's greatest achievements as governor. In fact, the July 6, 1992 *U.S. News & World Report* called ADFA, "a big factor behind Clinton's successful record as a jobs produc-

er — a core element of his claim to the presidency."
ADFA's purpose is to provide a source for long-term low-interest, and fixed-rate financing for businesses, housing and public facilities.

The organization pools the capital requests of private and public companies and organizations, then markets them as one large bond offering under the ADFA name. Not only are many fees avoided by the pooling, the interest rates are lower due to the agency's high bond rating. As one of the first agencies in the nation to develop an industrial bond pooling program, ADFA has a nationwide reputation for leading the way in innovative economic development and housing programs.

It also enables small businesses in Arkansas to participate in the bond market and brings down the net interest rate for borrowers in the state.

Reservations About the Arkansas Model

Some observers, however, have reservations about both the SDB and ADFA programs. Although the goal of increasing access to capital is commendable, some question the role of state government in controlling avenues to capital.

And, while it may work in the relatively small state of Arkansas, many fear that if a similar concept were applied nationally, it could lead to an industrial policy — which, by controlling access to capital, the government could dictate the "winners" and "losers" among businesses. This would diminish the role of the marketplace in the free enterprise system. Detractors, even in Arkansas, believe that programs like ADFA make getting financing a politically influenced process.

...Or Foe?

President Clinton's small business plan states, "I want a government that works with business to spur growth, create jobs and increase incomes."

Small business owners support growth, jobs and higher incomes but many fear that "a government that works with business" is campaign language which translates into "industrial policy" or a government that "interferes with business." Besides, small business owners do not want the federal government as a partner — they'd rather the government stay out of their way.

While President Clinton has a good small business record in Arkansas and seeks to support small business success on a national scale, in building a coalition during the presidential campaign he put himself at odds with small business on a number of important issues.

For those who laud his record as governor, perhaps the most confusing position candidate Clinton took during the campaign was his support for the federal repeal of the provision allowing states to have right-to-work laws. As governor of Arkansas, he presided over a right-to-work state, a fact touted in recruitment advertisements and materials produced during his administration.

Bill Clinton: Friend of Small Business?

So will President Clinton be a friend of small business, or a foe? The answer comes down to an argument between history and logic.

History reveals that as governor of Arkansas, Bill Clinton was a strong friend to small business.

Logic argues that many of his supporters will expect his continued support on specific issues that will hurt small businesses.

On this vital question, small business owners are hoping the words of Oliver Wendell Holmes contain the answer:

"A page of history is worth a volume of logic."

3

Small Business Issues Facing a New President

Following the heady days of campaign, victory, transition and inauguration, the reality of governing sets in. The challenge of sustaining economic growth — creating more and better jobs — is the new president's top priority, he has said time and again.

As has been shown, the role of small business is pivotal in any plan to get the economy growing in a sustained way. So one should expect that issues relating to small business will receive top billing in the early days of the new administration. However, few expect the issues to be resolved instantly. Indeed it could take two or three years for major legislative initiatives like health care reform to be fully debated and legislated.

During his campaign, President Clinton outlined numerous ideas related to problems affecting small business. However, few specifics emerged from his plans. This book was published on the eve of the new administration taking office, before priorities had been fully established and made public. However, the framework of the issues debate was shaping up.

Small business owners should be prepared to watch for,

study and respond to the details of these issues as they witness the debate unfold in the nation's capital.

A more detailed discussion of each issue's background and the president's views on them are presented in the following chapters. Here is an outline of some of the major issues to look for:

•Health Care Reform. A politically sensitive issue even before the campaign, health care reform constituted a chief plank in President Clinton's platform. The pressure will be on to find some means to provide health care insurance to the 33 to 37 million who do not have it and to stabilize the health care and insurance markets. The debate will be over three basic approaches: a single-payor (more-or-less nationalized) system of insurance, a private-and-public system that includes mandated employer-sponsored insurance, or a system that allows greater influence of market forces, competition and choice. Clinton will find support for many aspects of his plan, but small business will oppose bitterly mandated employer-sponsored coverage.

•Taxes, the Deficit and Economic Stimulation. In his campaign for president, Clinton ran against the budget deficit, while proposing potentially large new spending programs that will require additional revenue to fund. He proposed a new payroll tax for worker training, as well as changes in income tax rates and thresholds. There may well be efforts to raise the alternative minimum tax. In the area of spending, look for continued efforts to pass a balanced budget amendment and to approve presidential line-item vetoes.

To get the economy growing, the president must encourage the creation and expansion of small businesses. Clinton has pledged to increase access to capital and credit with, among other things, a new enterprise tax credit, community banks and micro-enterprise programs. He also promised to strengthen investment incentives and to work to reduce the federal deficit so credit can be more readily obtained.

•**Workplace and Labor.** As governor, Bill Clinton actively recruited business for Arkansas and was sympathetic to many concerns of business, such as right to work. However, he also wooed and won significant traditional Democratic support from labor with promises to sign legislation for family leave and against striker replacement. To keep the support of both sides, he must try to find a balance.

•**Regulation.** The passage of any law virtually guarantees creation of new regulations to implement it, so the regulatory burden can only increase – no matter who sits in the White House. It grew under the Bush administration, and will almost certainly grow under Clinton, despite his pledge to cut regulation by enforcing the Regulatory Flexibility Act of 1989.

•**Environment.** Thanks to Vice President Albert Gore's book, *Earth in the Balance,* the environment became a central focus of the campaign, and will continue to be so during the Clinton administration. Battles will likely focus on property rights vs. environmental impacts; just compensation of citizens and businesses affected by environmental regulation; and community rights to know more about potential environmental hazards. Small businesses will face greater regulation and monitoring in this area.

Government and Small Business

President Clinton will soon learn what all White House residents quickly discover: When it comes to legislation, the President proposes, but Congress disposes.

During 12 years of Republican administrations, Congress has developed an agenda of its own. At the same time, a process has emerged that perpetuates greater government involvement in the lives of all Americans.

In the past 20 years, a professional, unofficial civil service has arisen in Washington that transcends the electoral process. This group includes politicians and their staffs, departmental bureaucrats, lobbyists, self-appointed watchdogs and narrowly focused special interest groups. Each has an agenda to promote and most are insulated from the effects of periodic elections.

Partly in response to this situation, serving in Congress has become a full-time occupation. Twenty years ago,

Approaching the Issues

Congress worked from January to the Lincoln's Birthday recess, came back until summer, returned in September and October and adjourned before Thanksgiving.

Today, Congress is active year-round, either with committee work or full sessions. Activist politicians employ large staffs to formulate legislation or handle routine work while they pursue particular interests – their own re-election receiving top priority. However, the success of term limit initiatives in the November 3, 1992 elections may signal a coming change in the mind-set of professional politicians.

For the non-elected civil servants, success is measured by remaining in place. Display a justification for your existence and you can protect your career. The passage of a law creates or empowers a bureaucracy to implement it. Lobbyists try to repeal or modify it according to the desires of various interest or watchdog groups.

A new president may influence policy to some degree through political appointments, but even these do not guarantee fulfillment of a vision. At times, for example, the activist actions of Secretary of Labor Elizabeth Dole seemed out of step with the "get-the-government-off-the-backs-of-small-business" words of President Bush. The Environmental Protection Agency was similarly out of synch with Bush's stated agenda.

Clinton will enjoy a honeymoon, as most new presidents do. But having pledged to be an activist president who will present new programs within his first 100 days in office, the honeymoon could be brief.

Where Does Small Business Fit in This Process?

Washington insiders agree that small business owners can play an extremely influential role in determining policy in Washington. Small business represents a much broader spectrum of ideas than narrow special interest groups. Small business' concerns focus on broad issues that affect many citizens. Legislators want to know where small business stands on an issue, because that knowledge is a good measure of where the public interest lies.

Small business owners should be involved at every step of the legislative process – when bills are introduced, heard in sub-committees and committees, revised and amended, sent to the floor for action and passed on to the president. Individually and collectively, the voice of small business should be heard.

The following chapters are not intended as an exhaustive discussion of the major issues affecting small business in a Clinton administration. Rather, each will review a specific issue, recap likely Clinton and Congressional action, and will discuss its impact on small business.

Later chapters will examine what small business owners can do to help ensure they are heard, including aids for reaching specific lawmakers. Voting is only the first step; involvement must be continuing, unified and strategic if small business is to remain the backbone of the nation's economy.

4

Health Care: Healing A Sick System

Mandated Employer-sponsored Health Coverage
National Health Care Planning and Management
Managed Competition
Health Care Reform

Health care and the complex economic and public policy issues associated with it were a central focus of the 1992 presidential campaign. Each day, the American public heard horror stories concerning the millions of individuals without insurance coverage and the crisis of runaway medical costs.

But for small business owners, it's not just a campaign issue.

They are personally and painfully aware of the nation's health care problems because the debate over health care reform impacts them directly. Larger companies can usually self-insure to try to control costs and to insulate themselves from numerous state and federal regulatory requirements and mandated programs. That leaves small businesses as the primary customers in the health insurance policy market.

What they find in that market are highly volatile premiums; sudden cancellation of policies; a patchwork quilt of state and federally required benefits that prevent flexibility in insurance coverage and increase the cost of policies; unfair and discriminatory tax laws; the inability to implement cost control mechanisms such as managed care arrangements; and a general lack of willingness by anyone to impose meaningful cost controls.

In short, American small business owners see the current health care system nearly broken, with health care costs spiraling out of control. Rather than discard it for a nationalized system or impose mandated insurance coverage, however, they prefer to fix those elements that no longer work. Their ideal health care system would be based on free market principles and would assure that insurance is affordable, accessible, renewable and portable.

A survey of small business owners in 1986 revealed health care reform to be their number one concern. Surveyed again in 1992, they again ranked health care reform as their number one concern, twice the level of the next highest ranked issue, federal taxes on business.

The heart of the issue is cost. Between 1987 and 1991, the cost of health insurance for a single employee rose 79 percent; for family coverage, it rose 72 percent. A poll by Foster Higgins in 1991 showed the average per-employee cost of health insurance was more than $3,500. For small businesses the costs are even higher.

This is the bad news. The encouraging words, which

seldom are heard, are that since 1940, the number of people covered by public or private insurance has risen from 40 percent of the population to 84 percent. Some two-thirds of small businesses offer health insurance to employees, and most of those that do not would do so if they could afford it.

President Clinton vowed to send a health reform package to Congress within his first 100 days in office. He knows, however, the struggle over health care reform will be a long and difficult one. Small business owners will have a tremendous opportunity to be a part of the debate.

Although President Clinton has declared support for competition and cost controls, his ideas — as outlined during the campaign — would require all employers to purchase health insurance for their employees. He also endorsed the creation of a national health care board that would design benefits packages, set co-payments and deductibles, and impose a global budget (which would place a ceiling on total health care spending in the United States).

Whatever the shape of his final proposal, it will not have an easy passage. The past two sessions of Congress had dozens of health care proposals pending before them. Few of the bills, however, saw floor debate and none were put to a real vote. Health care affects so many groups that lobbying will be intense, prolonged and bitter.

Despite the complexities of the subject, small business owners need to learn as much as possible about it in the coming months to better understand the issues involved and how any given solution will affect them and their employees.

The Fight Against Mandated Employer-sponsored Health Insurance

Surveys show that 88 percent of small business owners oppose a federal mandate requiring employers to purchase health insurance for all employees. Mandated coverage would force many new and marginally profitable businesses to shut down. It would also significantly reduce the profitability of more established companies and inhibit their ability to expand and create jobs.

Small business owners can play a pivotal role in the final outcome of the debate over health care policy. As indicated earlier, they are the primary players in the insurance marketplace, so in reality, are the focus of the debate. (A measure of their strength was seen on the day President Clinton was elected. An NFIB-supported voter education campaign in California helped to defeat, by a margin of 68-32 percent, a ballot initiative mandating employer-sponsored insurance. The California experience suggests that when voters understand the negative impact mandated employer-sponsored insurance has on the creation of jobs, they do not support it.)

A president and Congress from the same party do not necessarily add up to mandated insurance, play-or-pay, or a single payor solution to health care reform. These issues are some of the most complex, far-reaching and deeply divisive ever to face Congress — and, indeed, the country. Small business owners — who create two-thirds of all new jobs and who will likely bear the brunt of any decision — need to speak up forcefully in this debate.

Repeatedly, surveys of small business owners have shown they want to return to free market principles to ensure the affordability, availability, renewability and portability of health insurance for themselves and their employees.

One of the difficulties with health care reform in the past has been the desire to implement radical, sweeping changes all at once. The very scope of these reforms has — so far, at least — ensured their failure in Congress.

A step-by-step approach is more reasonable and practical.

**Health Care Reform:
An Approach Supported
by Small Business**

There are a number of proposals that can be enacted a step at a time that will benefit small business and its employees in the long run by making health care insurance more affordable and accessible. These reforms are supported by NFIB.

Known collectively as small market health insurance reform, these positions include:

- **Pre-empt state health insurance benefit mandates and allow the insurance industry to develop affordable basic benefit packages.** These mandates alone can raise the cost of insurance 30 percent. Pre-empting these mandates would allow insurers to create competitive, low-cost basic policies that could be marketed nationally to new and less profitable employers. (A model for this is in the President's home state of Arkansas, a program he initiated and supported.)

- **Allow small businesses to form insurance purchasing groups.** Joining together to purchase health insurance, small businesses can significantly reduce administrative and medical costs through economies of scale and risk-sharing.

- **Expand and make permanent the tax deductibility of premiums from 25 percent to 100 percent for self-employed business owners such as sole proprietors, partnerships and S-corporations.** The Employee Benefits Research Institute estimated in 1990 that 21 percent of the self-employed were uninsured and that the number was increasing. This proposal would enable many of the 4.8 million uninsured self-employed to buy coverage for themselves and their nearly 5 million employees.

- **Restrict the pre-existing condition limitation.** If a person has previously been insured, they should be able to obtain insurance for their pre-existing condition if they change jobs or carriers.

•Institute rating bands to bring stability to insurance costs. Due to current insurance industry practices, small businesses experience highly volatile premium fluctuations. Rating bands would group similar types of businesses into blocks and would allow for no more than a 20-percent variance of insurance costs within a block. Also, premiums within a block could not rise more than 1.5 times the lowest premium for the first three years. Properly constructed, rating bands would enable small companies to plan for future premium changes.

•Guarantee renewability of health insurance policies and prohibit cancellation because of claims history. Insurers should not be allowed to cancel policies unless the insured has been flagrantly negligent in paying premiums or has engaged in fraudulent practices.

•Establish risk pools. Such pools spread the cost of covering the relatively small number of high-risk people in the population.

•Promote managed care and utilization review and pre-empt state anti-managed care laws. Managed care and utilization review are means of controlling costs — and raising the quality of care.

•**Educate health care consumers and implement cost-sharing.** Consumers need to be better informed so they can make intelligent choices in their health care. They need to know about provider fees, treatment protocols and quality so they can decide whether to accept or refuse treatments. Cost-sharing through higher deductibles and co-payments can act as an incentive for consumers to make sounder judgments before accessing health care services.

•**Reform medical malpractice laws.** A uniform statute of limitations, caps on damages, the use of practice guidelines as a defense, and eliminating the collateral source rule, among other reforms, would lower malpractice premiums and medical fees. They would also reduce the incidence of defensive medicine.

•**Simplify health insurance administration.** Reducing paperwork through uniform claims procedures and electronic filing of payments would markedly cut the cost of administering insurance.

•**Conduct outcomes research.** Information on the effectiveness of treatments will assist consumers in making health care choices.

The Health Care Debate: Understanding the Alternatives

Health care reform is one of the most complex challenges confronting the country today. It embraces many difficult financial, social, legal and ethical questions. Dozens of health care reform bills were introduced in the 101st and 102nd Congresses, each differing in the details of how it approached these questions. Beneath the details, however, lie three basic concepts — single-payor systems, play-or-pay, and managed competition.

Single-payor Health Care

A "single-payor" approach is, in effect, a nationalized health care plan. This would be the most radical solution to providing access for all citizens, and is least likely to gain widespread support in Congress. However, from its principles spring many of the elements that will be central to the health care debate. It should be noted that President Clinton does not advocate this solution.

In such a plan, the federal government could become a "single payor" of all health care costs, either directly or through state-administered programs. Or, Medicare could be expanded to include all citizens. Or, the government could both finance and provide services, such as is the case in Great Britain.

Canada has often been cited as a success story in single-payor or nationalized health care. Canada spends about 8 percent of its GNP on health care, as opposed to more than 12 percent in the United States. These figures are misleading, apple-and-orange comparisons. America has 1.2 times as many people over 65 as Canada; a teenage pregnancy rate 2.5 times that of Canada; twice the birth rate, twice the miscarriage rate and three times the abortion rate; and a crime rate far above that in Canada. The United States also spends much more on research and development than Canada.

The Canadian system is financed through stiff taxes. What its citizens get for their money is, in essence, rationed health care. In Newfoundland, there is a 10-week wait for mammograms; 6 to 10 months for hip replacements; 2 months for CAT scans; 2 to 5 months for PAP smears. U.S. hospitals along the border are filled with Canadian patients who could not afford to wait for heart surgery and other pressing care.

While he has said he favors competition within a budgeted structure, President Clinton's plan contains aspects of nationalized health care — a national health care board empowered to determine coverage, premiums, co-payments, deductibles and overall policy; a global annual budget for health care with spending caps; universal coverage and access; and limitations on duplicated technology and services.

Small business owners are on record as opposing any option that even hints of a nationalized health care system.

Play-or-Pay

One of the most-discussed offspring of mandatory employer-sponsored coverage is known as "play-or-pay." Essentially, employers would have to choose either to "play" — provide employee health insurance — or "pay" a 7- to 9-percent payroll tax (or fine or penalty) to fund a publicly sponsored program in which their employees would participate.

Play-or-pay translates to a regressive tax levied on those least able to pay. This is true whether the tax is "direct" in the form of an insurance premium or "indirect" as in a fine. It is true whether the burden falls on employees in the form of lower wages and fewer jobs, or on employers who would give up earnings to pay it.

A 1989 survey showed a direct link between business profitability and the availability of employee health insurance. The survey showed that 90 percent of business owners who took more than $70,000 out of their businesses offered insurance, while only a third of those taking out $20,000 or less provided such benefits.

According to the survey, if employers who currently do not provide health insurance to their employees were required to contribute $150 a month per employee for health insurance, 26.4 percent would close their businesses, and 23.9 percent would let all employees go and continue operating. Millions of employees would be forced into the public program as businesses closed or were forced to lay off workers.

If play-or-pay were enacted, the CONSAD Research Corporation predicts 9.1 million jobs would be at risk. The Congressional Joint Economic Committee predicted that 710,000 workers would lose their jobs in the first year of implementation. And the Employer Benefit Research Institute estimated that between 200,000 and 1.2 million workers could lose their jobs as a result of employer mandates.

The Joint Economic Committee also estimated that play-or-pay would cost nearly $90 billion in its first year, forcing employers to pay more than $42 billion in increased insurance premiums or tax penalties and costing taxpayers more than $44 billion in higher taxes or bigger budget deficits.

The net result of this approach would be to encourage most employers to opt for the government plan (pay) instead of private insurance (play) because, according to analysis, the government option will ultimately be offered at a less expensive rate.

Studies reveal that the outcome will be, in effect, a nationalized Medicare-style public insurance system with no mechanisms or incentives to control costs.

Managed Competition

As a candidate, President Clinton said he favored a "managed competition" approach to solving the health care crisis. He envisioned individuals and small businesses forming groups to purchase standardized, fairly inexpensive health care insurance. His vision is in line with several proposals floated in the 102nd Congress, including one from the Conservative Democratic Forum that received much interest.

Under this type of proposal, employers and other health care insurance purchasers could band together in health insurance purchasing cooperatives to realize economies of scale and risk-sharing. (You'll soon start hearing the shorthand acronym for these health plan purchasing cooperatives, HPPCs, or as they say in Washington, "Hippicks.") In a HPPC, employees and other individuals could choose among several types of plans. They would have incentives to choose the least expensive plan. For instance, they would be required to pay for coverage they chose that was above the standardized package. There would also be cost-sharing incentives to encourage wise use of health care services.

Accountable health plans would compete on the basis of the quality of care they delivered and the service they provided. As is the case in managed care arrangements, health care providers would have incentives to hold down costs and to be efficient in delivery of care. Managed competition requires outcomes research to be conducted and distributed to all beneficiaries.

From the small business perspective, managed competition has several attractive features:

•First, it allows market forces to control the cost of delivering health care. Groups of small employers and individuals, who cannot self-insure and thus comprise the bulk of the market for health care insurance, could realize potentially significant savings on premiums. Competing insurers would have strong incentives to provide affordable policies and to focus on quality. Health care providers also would have incentives to contain costs in order to compete for business.

• Second, it allows employees greater flexibility in the choice of health care plans.

• Third, it imposes a degree of cost control by capping the deduction of health care premiums and by requiring employees to share in the cost of insurance. Some models provide for employer contributions while others would require employees to pay most or all of the premiums. Employees would also likely have to meet deductibles and make co-payments.

The Clinton plan calls for a kind of managed competition, but envisions a single benefits package and community rating of premiums. Premiums would be deductible based on the lowest premium offered, which would likely lead to virtual uniformity of premiums regardless of efficiency. It is difficult to see how this arrangement would promote true competition except in the area of claims service and quality of providers in a plan — which could be measured only after several years of experience.

The Clinton Health Care Plan and Small Business

First, and foremost, small businesses greatly oppose

President Clinton's call for universal employer-sponsored health care insurance. They see it as a fundamental threat to their ability to survive. They will oppose him on this point with all resources available.

However, there are aspects of his plan on which the president will find small businesses' enthusiastic support.

President Clinton made health care a central issue of his campaign, addressing it frequently in speeches and also in his book, *Putting People First*, where he declared, "Health care should be a right, not a privilege."

Right or privilege, health care is expensive and getting more so. Since 1970, health care expenditures have risen 60 percent faster than general inflation. According to government data, Americans spent more than $738 billion dollars on health care in 1991 and an estimated $809 billion in 1992 — more than 15 percent of the Gross National Product, or $3,000 for every citizen. The Health Care Financing Administration has predicted health care spending will absorb 16.4 percent of GNP by the end of the decade.

Private insurance, much of it through employers, paid 33 percent of the bills, out-of-pocket payments accounted for 20 percent, and public programs such as Medicaid and Medicare paid 42.4 percent, according to *Health Care Financing Review*.

During the campaign, President Clinton said the goal of his administration will be to control health care costs so they rise no faster than wages. He estimated this will save Americans some $700 billion by the year 2000.

While its details are still being worked out, he has said his health care plan would address guaranteed universal coverage, cost control and preserving the best of the U.S. health care system.

Surveys of small business owners show they are nervous about many of the core elements of the Clinton plan. There is concern that under its apparently free-market, competitive clothing lurks a *de facto* nationalized health care wolf. They are leery of the creation of a new, large government bureaucracy and also of the unknown costs involved, both for insurance packages and also for possible new taxes to help fund the plan.

Based on his book and on a campaign white paper issued in late September 1992, following is an outline of the chief features of President Clinton's health care plan and the response of small business:

Guaranteed Coverage for Working Families

Clinton Plan

• All employers would be required to provide health insurance to all workers and their families. Presently about 85 percent of all employees and their families have coverage through their employers. Employers could buy coverage either directly from insurers or through a publicly sponsored purchasing group. Employer requirements would be phased in, with the smallest businesses coming into the system last.

Nonworkers and their families would have private coverage through the publicly sponsored purchasing groups and would pay a portion of the costs based on a sliding scale.

Small Business Response

A key element of President Clinton's plan, mandated coverage would require all employers to offer health insurance as a benefit for full- and part-time employees. But since 15 percent of the 33 to 37 million uninsured are also unemployed, mandated insurance would provide only a partial solution.

In fact, mandated coverage could aggravate this situation, by forcing employers faced with stiff additional costs to lay off workers or even close their businesses. Mandated coverage is essentially a play-or-pay approach, and would have the same disastrous results for millions of employers and employees. As discussed earlier, President Clinton's employer-sponsored mandates could lead by default to nationalized health care.

Mandated employer-provided health insurance also denies business owners the flexibility to adapt insurance benefits to the needs of their employees and of their individual enterprises. Mandated coverage ultimately would inhibit business owners from expanding staff, production capacity and employee benefits.

Changes in Tax Laws

Clinton Plan

•Tax credits would be made available for companies needing help to offset the costs of providing insurance. The self-employed insurance tax deduction would be raised from 25 percent to 100 percent on a phased-in basis.

Small Business Response

Small businesses and self-employed people enthusiastically support 100-percent deductibility of health insurance premiums. Generally, they also like the idea of being able to form groups to purchase coverage, but only if participation is voluntary.

National Health Care Board

Clinton Plan

•Central to the president's health care package would be the creation of a national health care board. The board, composed of health care providers, consumers, business, labor and other interested parties, would design a benefits package, set national deductibles and co-payments and generally control implementation of health care policy. The national board would impose global *health care budgeting by establishing national and state spending caps — price controls — on health care costs. Tied to some measure, such as the Gross Domestic Product, these cost controls would, in theory, keep health care costs from rising faster than wages, as they do now. It is not clear what would happen if spending exceeds the cap.*

Small Business Response

While they agree that health care costs are out of control, small business owners have absolutely no faith in the government's ability to control them. They point to the problems with Medicare, which, despite price controls, is the fastest-growing domestic program. Price controls have failed to control costs in nationalized health care systems such as in Germany and Canada.

There is also concern over how insurers can compete and contain costs if each health plan must offer the same package, deductibles and co-payments, based on the same premium structure for every community.

Employers who offer health insurance to their employees know all too well the pitfalls of mandates. State governments impose various coverage mandates — some 900 nationwide — requiring certain types of coverage in all employee health insurance, except for larger employers' plans that "self-insure" health care coverage. Covered services run the gamut from basic medical care to herbal medicine, in-vitro fertilization, smoking cessation and hair transplants. Since large companies that self-insure can avoid ERISA requirements, small businesses bear the brunt of these mandates.

The net effect is to raise insurance costs and limit business owners' flexibility to choose plans that fit their employee needs. As many as 8.5 million Americans have been priced out of the health insurance market by costly state mandates, according to the National Center for Policy Analysis.

Health Insurance and Care Networks

Clinton Plan

- *The Clinton plan calls for the creation of local health networks, composed of insurers, hospitals and a variety of health care providers, to permit sharing of resources and to eliminate duplication of services and technology. This plan would require changes in certain antitrust provisions.*

Small Business Response

Small business owners generally support the concept of being able to form groups to purchase health insurance. They also believe that allowing health care providers to join together in networks could help control costs and make health care delivery more efficient. These concepts are part of the managed competition approach, with one quite crucial difference — managed competition should not mandate that employers provide insurance coverage for employees.

Cost Controls

Clinton Plan

•The policies created under a national health board would include deductibles and co-payments to encourage cost-awareness and cost-sharing among consumers. A national global budget would be set for total health care spending. Health networks would receive "capitation fees" — fixed funds for each consumer's total health care. These limits would be intended to encourage the networks to control costs. He also pledged to seek an end to "prescription drug price gouging" by eliminating tax breaks for pharmaceutical companies that raise prices at a rate greater than inflation. Community health care solutions, such as school-based clinics and health centers in poorly served areas, would be expanded to provide easier and less costly access to care. Preventive and primary care would be emphasized as less costly than curative care.

Small Business Response

Small business owners endorse the cost-containment principles behind deductibles and co-payments. Some studies, such as the Rand Health Insurance Experiment conducted by the Rand Corporation in the 1970s, indicate that people tend to use medical care services more when they have to pay little or nothing.

As for capitation fees, this is just another term for price controls on a more local level than a national health care budget.

Small business owners would generally support efforts to contain health care costs in any sector, including new technology and drugs. There is concern, however, that such measures should not affect the overall quality of care.

In many areas, hospital emergency rooms provide a great deal of basic health services for the uninsured and poor. If more cost-effective alternatives to this most expensive kind of medical care could be found, they would benefit the patients, the over-burdened hospitals and all payors of medical costs. The same can be said for better preventive and primary care. The questions that small business owners ask are — How will it be done? And who will pay for it?

New Rules for Insurance Companies

Clinton Plan

•The Clinton plan calls for a comprehensive benefits package for preventive and primary care as determined by the National Health Care Board. This basic package

would include full protection in case of illness and also freedom for consumers to choose where to receive care. The plan also calls for the establishment of publicly sponsored insurance purchasing groups composed of small businesses and individuals. These would encourage competition among health networks to offer quality plans at the lowest possible cost in order to acquire customers. Pre-existing condition exclusions would be prohibited. Premiums would be "community rated" to prevent insurers from charging more because of employer size, health conditions or gender. Claim filing would be unified and simplified to reduce administrative costs. There would be a crackdown on fraud. Medical malpractice law would be reformed to reduce the practice of costly defensive medicine and lower malpractice insurance costs.

Small Business Response

Small business owners are not sure how the Clinton plan will foster competition among insurers, if all policies are the same. Based on their experience with state mandates on coverage, they also worry what will comprise a "basic" package and how much it will cost. By eliminating flexibility in designing coverage, the basic policy could be inadequate for many businesses and more than needed for others. Business owners are also concerned about community rating, which could increase the cost of health insurance for those with relatively healthy employees.

However, small business owners support eliminating preexisting condition exclusions, which currently help make obtaining coverage difficult and expensive. Any improvement in administrative procedures is needed, as is the reduction of fraud and an easing of the malpractice law burden.

Other Initiatives

Clinton Plan

- The Clinton plan includes expanded health education and encouragement of personal responsibility in health care choices. He also has proposed issuance of "smart cards" containing computer-readable personal medical information. In addition, the plan calls for increased long-term care benefits for the elderly and disabled through Medicare and more access to home- and community-based care, with funding flexible enough to permit such freedom of choice.

Small Business Response

A better educated public should be able to make wiser choices about health care and about lifestyles that can affect their need for health care. Providing information would ensure accountability within the system and make deceptive or aggressive rating practices and defensive medicine less likely to occur. Overall, there needs to be a reduction in the amount of paperwork flowing through the system. The "smart cards" will make health care delivery and administration more efficient — although concerns have been raised about privacy and confidentiality.

In making long-term care more available and flexible under Medicare, President Clinton could open the door to huge increases in federal spending. The elderly are the fastest-growing segment of the population and consume huge amounts of health care services. Home or community care might be less expensive than hospital or skilled nursing homes, but this requires further study.

Conclusion:
Small Business Owners
Can Make A Difference

Health care reform presents President Clinton and Congress with a challenging high-wire act. One slip could initiate devastating economic, social and, of course, political consequences.

Small businesses account for two-thirds of the new jobs created in the United States. Uninsured workers are employed primarily by the newest, smallest or least profitable of these businesses. Often the business owner is uninsured as well.

Their reasons for not providing health insurance are almost always economic. If they could make it available, they would. But faced with the choice of offering an extremely expensive benefit or staying in business, they choose the latter.

Reform plans that mandate employer-sponsored insurance could force up to half those business owners to shut down or lay off some or all of their employees. Even with tax breaks, many employers would be unable to meet the cost of insurance premiums or payroll taxes to support public insurance programs.

President Clinton has indicated he supports mandated coverage, phased in over several years so that the smallest businesses are affected last. His plan offers no assurances that costs can be contained or that premiums will not remain dangerously high for small businesses. And, by empowering a national board to impose standards, premiums and global spending limits on health care costs, his plan drastically curtails the role of competition and market forces.

He and small business are in agreement that there needs to be 100-percent deductibility of health insurance premiums for the self employed and that medical malpractice and insurance industry practices must be reformed. They concur that insurance should be portable and renewable.

It will take time for a Clinton plan to make its way through Congress. There will be support and opposition from many groups on all sides of the issue. As the group at the very heart of the issue, small business owners cannot afford to let health care reform be decided without them.

Health Care

Each and every owner of a small business should follow the issue closely and let their representative and senators know where they stand.

It's an issue too important to ignore.

5

Taxes

Payroll Taxes
Income Taxes: Personal & Corporate
Estate Taxes
VAT or National Sales Tax

A nationwide exit poll conducted for the television networks by Voter Research and Surveys asked voters whether they would rather have "government provide more services but cost more in taxes" or "government cost less in taxes but provide fewer services." Fifty-four percent of voters favored less government and lower taxes.

This sentiment of the American voter is even more evident among the owners of small businesses who, when surveyed with a similar question by NFIB, responded overwhelmingly that the federal government should not raise taxes, but should operate within the framework of the revenues it currently collects.

As a candidate, President Clinton outlined a number of tax-raising proposals, some of which became a central focus of the campaign. Others — perhaps because of their complexity and apparently narrow focus — flew below the radar of intense scrutiny by the media. These proposals, some of which will be discussed in more detail in the "Income Tax" section of this chapter, include:

- *Raising the Alternative Minimum Tax*
- *Preventing tax fraud on unearned income for the wealthy*
- *Limiting corporate deductions for executive salaries to $1 million*
- *Ending incentives for opening plants overseas*
- *Increasing fines and taxes for corporate polluters*
- *Eliminating tax deductions for lobbying expenses*

Small business owners are — and should be — concerned that the balance sheet on Clinton's plan for taxes and spending just does not add up when one compares how much revenue will be needed to fund programs he has promised with how little revenue can be generated from the sources he has outlined. Therefore, if the promised programs are enacted, one of two results is inevitable: taxes will be raised or the deficit will continue to grow. Or both.

Payroll Taxes

Payroll taxes are the most difficult for small business to afford. They are taxes that must be paid whether a business is profitable or not. They are particularly devastating on new companies struggling to become profitable. Far from being an "income tax," payroll taxes are imposed on and collected from a new entrepreneur within weeks of opening a new business. They are taxes that must be paid, often before the company has even mailed an invoice or collected a penny in revenue. They start being paid the day a business owner hires his or her first employee and never stops.

Income taxes are based upon how much a business or individual earns each year. Payroll taxes, however, are regressive. They ignore the ability of a business or individual to pay. Since small businesses typically earn very little in the first few years and are usually labor-intensive, payroll taxes are disproportionately burdensome to them. In fact, a decade-old study revealed that payroll taxes often exceed 80 percent of a small business' total tax burden.

Yet payroll-based taxes are very attractive to a Congress trying to raise revenue because they are managed and collected by a middle man — the employer — who must contribute, in effect, "matching funds" on employee tax withholdings. No other form of federal tax raises so much revenue so fast.

No wonder small business owners oppose, with great passion, any form of new payroll tax — whether it is called a tax or is falsely labeled with a name like "mandated benefit."

During his campaign, Clinton called for at least one such *de facto* payroll tax to raise funds for a worker training program (described in greater detail in Chapter 8).

Although it was not heavily promoted as a "payroll tax," even its strongest proponents admit it walks like a payroll tax and quacks like a payroll tax. It will be extracted from employers almost on day one, long before most start-up companies become profitable. Rather than accomplishing a worthy goal, this new payroll tax would punish the very individuals it is designed to aid: low-wage workers.

Income Taxes: Personal & Corporate

Perhaps the most publicized tax-related topic during the presidential campaign was Clinton's call for raising income taxes on the "top 2 percent" of wage earners.

Despite the limitations Clinton has given to those who will be taxed, small business owners (who average taking home less than $40,000 annually in profits and salary from their businesses) fully expect Congress to propose tax increases that affect more than just the well-to-do.

Raising rates on income levels well below households with incomes of $200,000 is anticipated. And raising corporate rates will be championed by some on Capitol Hill who were major supporters of President Clinton's election.

New Revenue Sources Likely in a Clinton-103rd Congress Tax Plan

To get a feel for a likely revenue-raising package to be seen in the 103rd Congress, a small business owner need look no further than the "Tax Fairness and Economic Growth Bill of 1992." This legislation was passed by both the House and Senate during the final days of the 102nd Congress but vetoed after the election by former President Bush because it raised taxes over a five-year period by an estimated $93.5 billion.

Instead of Clinton's proposed income levels of $200,000 (household) and $150,000 (individual), this Congressionally backed plan added a fourth individual rate bracket of 35 percent beginning at taxable income of $85,000 (single), $145,000 (joint) and $125,000 (head of household).

In addition to the Clinton-supported 10 percent surtax on incomes over $1 million and the elimination of corporate deductions related to CEO salaries over the $1 million level, this legislation included limitations on itemized deductions and a phase-out of personal exemptions for high-income taxpayers.

In addition to these changes, other sources for revenue in a Clinton plan could likely include the extension of the "95 percent test" for corporate estimated tax payments and making permanent the individual estimated tax "safe harbor" at 115 percent. These changes would force some small businesses to choose between overpaying their taxes or hiring an accountant to constantly monitor what the business is earning.

Look also for inclusion of a measure to extend depreciation on real estate from 31.5 to 40 years on non-residential property and from 27.5 to 31 years on residential property.

Another provision will likely be the increase in required miles for eligibility to deduct moving expenses.

The bill also will likely require the amortization of intangible assets.

A wild card in the tax-raising game is the corporate tax rate. If President Clinton's individual tax increase bill passes in 1993, it will be the second increase in personal rates in three years. A signal that raising corporate rates will be considered will come when "unidentified White House and Capitol sources" begin being quoted as saying, "corporations need to pay their fair share of taxes."

The Hidden Cost of Raising the Alternative Minimum Tax

A proposal to raise the "Alternative Minimum Tax" is also included among the tax proposals Clinton outlined in his book, *Putting People First*.

The tax, enacted as a part of the 1986 Tax Reform Act, was designed to improve the fairness of income tax by ensuring that corporate and individual taxpayers cannot reduce their tax liability to zero by combining tax preferences through the use of exclusions, deductions or credits.

One result of the tax measure is higher accounting, legal and administrative costs for high-income individuals and corporations. Because the minimum tax is required whenever it is greater than the regular tax, many taxpayers must engage in tax planning and tax computations under both the minimum and regular tax provisions.

By raising the floor of the Alternative Minimum Tax, even if it still affects only a few small business owners, the closing of the gap between the minimum tax and the regular tax would mean that a growing number of taxpayers will have to bear the extra costs associated with tax planning, preparation and filing.

Estate Taxes

Across this country, one hears tragic stories of how a family farm or business, born and built through the rugged determination, unyielding faith and ceaseless work of its founder, must be sold or broken up upon his or her death, due to the burden of a confiscatory estate tax structure.

The threat to small business of current estate tax laws can best be described by hearing, in his own words, the situation of the president and chief executive officer of a successful auto parts distribution company in the president's home town of Little Rock, Ark.

E. Fletcher Lord Jr. and his brother own slightly over 52 percent of Crow-Burlingame Company, a Little Rock auto parts business their grandfather started in 1919:

> "My grandfather died at 84, 45 years after founding the company. The entire time he was active in the company, most of its earnings were plowed back to finance future growth. Auto parts businesses require a lot of capital to support the large inventories required to provide parts coverage in the automotive aftermarket. For that reason, the size of the inventories greatly inflate the value of such a business for estate tax purposes.
>
> "When my grandfather died, it was thought that my grandmother might live several years past him, and his estate left enough to her to provide for her needs. She died 11 months later. In effect, all that was left to her was taxed twice.
>
> "Although my grandfather planned well and was frugal, after paying the taxes on both of my grandparents' estates, the family had virtually nothing left but company stock. Everything else had to be sold to pay the estate taxes.
>
> "My dad had been working for the company over 20 years when my grandfather died. Today he is 84, and my mom died two years ago. Although he will pass on less than one-third of the stock that my grandfather did, it will take all of his assets, his lump sum pension, his investments and his home to raise enough money to pay estate taxes. The best guess is that my brother and I will still need to chip in some of our own money to pay the taxes in order to keep the stock in the family.

"Today, it's my generation's turn to try to pass our business on to the next generation. My brother and I pay ourselves modest salaries, and our total compensation is in line with norms for our kind of business and other distribution companies of our size. There is not much room for additional salaries to plan for estate taxes.

"With the current tax laws there is no way for my family to move our ownership of our business to the next generation. I cannot afford to carry any more insurance to protect my stock and I cannot afford to save enough over the years to pay the tax. My family will lose our majority control of our company if my children have to redeem stock to pay the estate taxes.

"If either my brother or I die prematurely, it is entirely possible that the company will be in jeopardy of survival at that time, let alone pass to a new generation.

"I feel that our family has been a responsible member of the community, managed our business affairs well, been one of the more successful companies of our type in the country, but unfortunately that is not enough to survive estate taxes. My feeling is that by confiscating the assets of small farms and businesses, the country is eating its own seed corn. In the longer term, the country is better served by helping small business pass from generation to generation and encouraging their growth through its tax laws, than the short-term effect of raising more revenue up front."

When the owner of a family business or farm dies, the value of the enterprise is added to the owner's estate and taxed, after exemptions, at rates as high as 50 percent. As a result of this excessive tax, many family businesses must be sold just to pay the tax collector — and a business that may have been in the family for generations is lost.

In 1981, Congress provided an exemption from estate tax for the first $600,000 in a person's estate, but this exemption is inadequate when fixed assets, such as building and equipment, are involved. In addition, the real value of this exemption has declined due to inflation.

Few small businesses or farms can survive after paying up to 50 percent of their value to the federal government in taxes.

Despite this, there are those in Congress who still support lowering the $600,000 exemption as a means to raise more taxes. Such Congressional actions make small business owners believe the government is the enemy.

Small business owners need Congress and President Clinton to change the nation's estate tax laws so that closely held businesses and farms may be passed on intact without estate tax consequences if the business is kept in operation by the heirs. If the business is sold or liquidated, it should be taxed at rates no higher than ordinary income is taxed.

This would prevent those inheriting a small business or farm from being forced to sell or liquidate it in order to pay the estate taxes. Those working for small family farms and businesses will not face losing their jobs and the businesses can continue contributing to local economies.

VAT or National Sales Tax

Although it was not a part of President Clinton's campaign tax plan, a "value added tax" (VAT) or a related national sales tax might show up as part of a tax package originating on Capitol Hill during his first term in office.

A value added tax is a consumption tax imposed at each level of production; that is, the tax is imposed on the value added to a product by the manufacturer, the wholesaler and finally the distributor. The cumulative tax ultimately is passed on to the consumer of the product. A national sales tax would operate in a manner similar to state sales taxes.

Previous Congresses have considered several VAT proposals but none has been voted upon. Small business owners oppose both a national sales tax and a VAT. Either approach would create a new, complex system of raising additional revenue for the federal government. These taxes are hidden in the cost of goods and can be increased with impunity. Finally, even more than most new laws, they will create a nightmare of new paperwork and administrative problems for small business owners.

6

The Budget Deficit

Deficit Reduction
Balanced Budget Amendment/Budget Reform
The Line Item Veto

According to the Office of Management and Budget, at the end of fiscal 1992, the gross federal debt was estimated to total over $4 trillion. Due to record peacetime deficit spending, that's a 50 percent increase since 1988. When asked in 1991 whether Congress should focus its attention on deficit reduction, domestic programs or foreign affairs, 87 percent of small business owners surveyed said deficit reduction.

Small business owners have repeatedly and vocally supported balancing the federal budget and taking strong steps to curb federal spending. In fact, a recent survey of 5,000 small business owners revealed 72 percent would prefer cuts in the federal deficit to cuts in taxes. They heartily oppose raising taxes to reduce the deficit, urging spending cuts instead.

During the campaign, President Clinton said only the wealthy and foreign corporations doing business in the U.S. would bear additional tax burdens. But concern remains that the numbers won't add up — that there simply are not enough wealthy people to generate the kind of revenue he envisions.

Deficit Reduction: Why Care?

The federal government has incurred budget deficits since the beginning of our nation, although not on the scale seen in recent years. Since there have always been deficits, why should there be such concern now?

Deficits restrict access to capital by businesses, large and small. President Clinton acknowledged this in the campaign. He noted that the amount of outstanding commercial and industrial loans has dropped by $50 billion since 1991, and that for the first time since 1965, banks are investing more money in government securities than in loans to businesses. The capital needs of most small business owners are modest, but they are real and they usually relate to job formation. The deficit makes it difficult for them to find financing to go into business, expand or innovate.

More important, small business owners are concerned about the debt and its legacy to their children. If the debt had been called in the day after the election in 1992, every adult and child in the nation would have had to pay $16,000 to retire it. Obviously, that amount increases with each passing day. This way of running a government offends the instincts of small business owners. They worry that the ever expanding national debt will make it much more difficult for their children to continue the business or start a new one.

Balanced Budget Amendment/Budget Reform

The legacy of Ross Perot and the bitter budget battles of the Bush years will likely result in a debate and Congressional vote on a Constitutional amendment requiring a balanced federal budget. Deficit spending is bitterly opposed by American small business owners. They know firsthand the daily pressure of operating within one's means. Nothing galls them more than to see their elected officials appear not to have the discipline to solve the deficit problem and to attack the crisis of a national debt seemingly out of control.

In a recent survey, small business owners support a balanced budget amendment 2-to-1 if, and only if, it contains a limitation against raising taxes to match higher federal spending.

That's because small business owners know by common sense what The Congressional Joint Economic Committee's figures reveal: every time Congress increases taxes $1, spending increases by $1.59.

During the campaign, President Clinton proudly claimed he was the only candidate who had balanced a government budget, indeed 11 of them. But it is important to keep in mind that, in Arkansas, the legislature and chief executive are legally bound by the state constitution to have a balanced budget.

It is also important to remember that it takes time to amend the Constitution. A balanced budget amendment potentially would affect all citizens and groups, so the struggle over such an amendment would likely be fierce.

Besides the balanced budget amendment debate, there also will be much discussion of budget reform to prevent government from incurring deficits. Small business owners support enforcing annual spending caps built into the Gramm-Rudman-Hollings Deficit Reduction Act.

They also favor taking steps to restrain automatic spending increases in politically sensitive domestic entitlement programs. For example, Medicare is the fastest-growing domestic program, despite efforts to impose cost limits. Medicaid and other public health care programs are also driving up the deficit.

Line Item Veto

"To eliminate pork-barrel projects and cut government waste, we will ask Congress to give the president the line item veto," Clinton promised in *Putting People First*.

Although most governors have the power to veto individual projects or budget items, the president cannot. Recognizing this, Congress typically adds pet projects on to other, more important legislation, virtually daring the president to veto. Presidents have often sought to correct this frustrating situation.

A line item veto with a "simple majority" override will likely gather support early in the 103rd Congress.

7

The Clinton Plan to Encourage Small Business Creation and Growth and a Few More Ideas

"America needs a new approach to economics that will give new hope to our people and breathe new life into the American Dream," President Clinton said during his campaign. "We need a new national strategy that will reward work and those who play by the rules, that will expand opportunity for small business and entrepreneurs."

Small business owners agree with the president: a new approach is necessary to stem the decline in opportunity created by past governmental actions. Small business stands ready to support the president on his proposals which truly enable them to create new jobs. Proposals which free them from excessive regulatory burden, help them have access to capital, reward them for investing in new plant and equipment. Proposals which, as he says, "reward work and those who play by the rules."

While he did not detail the specifics of each facet of the plan, as a candidate, President Clinton unveiled a small business plan to encourage the creation and growth of enterprises. Small business owners do not necessarily agree with each point of his plan.

Clinton said his plan will:

• Provide a new enterprise tax credit that allows a 50 percent tax exclusion for those who take risks by making long-term investments in new businesses.

• Work with the private sector to create a national network of 100 community development banks and 1,000 microenterprise programs to provide capital and technical assistance to individuals who want to start or expand small businesses.

• Explore means of allowing pension funds to invest a greater portion of their portfolios in long-term venture and seed capital investments, while ensuring the security and safety of members' retirement investments.

• Direct banking regulatory agencies to review federal regulations, examination procedures and loan classification standards in an effort to increase banks' lending activity to small business.

• Explore new ways to "securitize" bank loans to small businesses into debt securities that can be sold in secondary markets, with techniques like those used for home mortgages and other asset-backed securities. Such "securitization" would free up bank capital for further small business lending.

•Increase opportunities and assure equal opportunity for qualified small business and community banks to access public equity markets. Support and further extend the recent Securities and Exchange Commission proposals to simplify registration requirements, reduce the costs and enhance the ability of small businesses to make Initial Public Offerings, while ensuring that adequate safeguards exist for investors.

•Modify, for small businesses only, the recent Financial Accounting Standards Board proposals on current accounting of the future value of executive stock options to support management's long-term commitment to the business.

•Strengthen investment incentives by providing a targeted investment tax credit, making permanent the research and development tax credit, and creating comprehensive enterprise zones.

As a candidate, Bill Clinton said the goal of government policy should be to assure viable private enterprises do not fail because they can't get capital or credit.

"Financial institutions should help create jobs and restore healthy economic growth," he said.

A Few More Suggestions

While they are not a part of the Clinton plan, here are some ideas supported by small business which could help encourage the establishment and growth of enterprises and new jobs:

- Issue new simple rules for the creation of S-corporations. S-corporations were created to help small business owners obtain the protection of a corporation without having to comply with the complicated rules of a C-corporation. Unfortunately, Congress and the IRS have made it increasingly difficult for S-corporations to operate. New simple rules for small S-corporations should be written to allow even the smallest business to have access to corporate form.

- Create a corporate tax bracket for businesses earning below $25,000 and, like low income individuals, offer them a zero tax rate if they reinvest the money in the business. Like individuals, if a company is new and barely profitable, or is struggling to stay in business, it shouldn't have to pay a tax on a slight profit the company retains to help it get going or get back on its feet.

The Clinton Plan for Stimulating Small Business

•In addition to an investment tax credit, allow small companies the opportunity to accelerate the expensing of investment in equipment. Increase the cap on the total amount they can expense in one year. This would not only help small businesses, it would encourage investment which immediately will ripple throughout the economy.

•Simplify tax returns for small businesses. Create an EZ tax form for businesses like the individual 1040EZ.

•Expand the types of small businesses which may utilize cash accounting for the reporting of taxable income.

8

Labor and the Workplace

Worker Training
Minimum Wage
Labor Law Reform
Striker Replacement
Right-To-Work
Child Labor
Family Leave
Davis-Bacon
OSHA Reform

President Bill Clinton knows from experience the economic benefits of a pro-business environment as it relates to the workplace. As governor of a right-to-work state, Clinton saw job growth surge 11.8 percent in the past four years. This job-growth record in Arkansas against the national trend of job loss helped put him in the White House.

Small business owners hope he will bring this experience to Washington to create a pro-business climate on a national scale.

However, part of the coalition that elected him, led by big labor, has quite a different agenda. If this coalition is allowed to control labor and workplace policy, small business owners face the prospect of increased governmental intrusion into the workplace. This intrusion could include new laws mandating costly and inflexible employee benefits, regulations changing the balance between employer and employee rights, and legislation that could lead to a resurgence of the power of organized labor. Each of these intrusions would hurt small business' ability to create jobs.

Big Labor's Support of President Clinton

Organized labor is loudly claiming ownership of the Clinton victory. The headline of the Nov. 9, 1992, post-election issue of *AFL-CIO News* declared "Labor Shares Clinton Victory." The article claimed that Clinton's victory was "boosted by intense labor efforts to turn out the union vote, which helped to decide the election in as many as 11 crucial battleground states, including Ohio, New Jersey and Michigan."

The article explained how unions backed the ticket: "The Clinton-Gore victory capped a vigorous effort by the AFL-CIO Committee on Political Education that was perhaps unprecedented in its intensity." Activities included the distribution of millions of pieces of campaign literature and a program which saw more than 300,000 volunteers nationwide getting out the vote for the Clinton ticket.

In addition, the Clinton-Gore campaign received an

overwhelming majority of labor union funds contributed. Small business owners can be assured that big labor will work hard to see that this political support will not go unnoticed or unrewarded.

The possible changes in labor relations and in the workplace over the next four years are likely to increase the cost of doing business and to inhibit the creation of jobs. They could also threaten the ability of small businesses to manage their work forces and to provide flexible benefits. It is therefore critical for small business owners to know what will probably be considered in the coming years regarding workplace and labor-related issues.

Worker Training

Small business owners know the value of a well-trained work force. Overwhelmingly, they provide some form of training for their employees, typically investing a significant amount of their own time providing on-the-job training with real tasks. This internal, individualized training makes for more skilled workers. But, because it is internal training often conducted by the owner, it is not an expense that is tracked or documented in any way. Under a plan proposed by President Clinton, however, the federal government would mandate ongoing worker training expenditures for all businesses.

On the campaign trail, President Clinton proposed requiring businesses either to spend 1.5 percent of their payrolls on continuing education and training for all workers, or to pay a comparable amount into a government fund. In turn, the fund would finance job training.

Government mandated training is bad for business and for the workers its advocates claim it will help. Most small business owners provide a large amount of training designed around the individual worker, training that harder to place workers — the elderly, youth, immigrant and displaced workers — need the most. The government mandate robs the owner of this individualized training and requires him or her to pay into a fund to provide advanced training for people already in the work force.

President Clinton's training mandate is a payroll tax and as such, it is a direct tax on jobs. Put simply, when the cost of payroll is calculated in planning for raises, increasing benefits or adding additional workers, a payroll tax for training will reduce the raise an employee may get, the number of benefits offered and hiring of new employees.

Under President Clinton's plan, employers would have to spend the required amount on training or pay it into a government fund that would finance job training. Small business owners have no faith in the government's ability to efficiently manage what would be an enormous and complex undertaking. Besides the obvious waste involved, it would put the funds under political influence.

Such a tax implies also the possibility of government targeting certain industries or geographic areas for training funds. This would result in the taxing of all for the benefit of a select few.

If training is going to be a government program, instead of government mandates, small businesses favor incentives, such as a tax credit for the training of new workers. Business owners already see training as a good investment. Instead of penalizing new employment, a tax credit would encourage employers to add workers and retrain those already on the payroll, which would be more efficient and more fair to everyone, especially the employee.

Minimum Wage

Small businesses are much more labor intensive than their large business counterparts. Overwhelmingly, people are a small business' most valuable — and most expensive — resource. Small businesses are among the largest employers of minimum wage earners, so any changes in minimum wage standards dramatically affect their ability to create jobs.

After heated debate on the issue as well as a presidential veto on earlier legislation, Congress amended the Fair Labor Standards Act in 1989. The legislation did more than raise the minimum wage from $3.35 in 1989 to the $4.25 it is today. It included a teenage limited training wage, an increased tip credit and a higher small business exemption.

The efforts during the 102nd Congress to raise the minimum wage failed despite attempts by some of its leaders. Edward Kennedy (D-Mass.), chairman of the Senate

Labor and Human Resources Committee, issued a statement March 28, 1992, that read, "Just to restore the ground lost during the Reagan years, the minimum wage should be $5.15 an hour today, not $4.25. I intend to do all I can to see that Congress closes the gap in 1992, and ends this continuing exploitation of the working poor."

Most observers of Capitol Hill anticipate a strong, coordinated effort by organized labor and Congressional liberals to increase the minimum wage further during President Clinton's first year in office. It is believed that legislation will include an immediate increase in the wage, possibly to $6.25, combined with an indexing measure that will automatically raise it with inflation. In his campaign outline, Bill Clinton called for an increase in the minimum wage to keep pace with inflation. Like other seemingly "no cost" government mandates, it will actually inhibit small businesses' ability to create jobs and will cost all consumers.

Proponents of raising the minimum wage almost always speak of the need to help the plight of the working poor. However, a closer examination of the work force shows that minimum wage earners are not necessarily the working poor.

A minimum wage earner working year-round as the sole support for a family is a rare exception to the rule, comprising about 10 percent of the total minimum wage work force. According to the Bureau of Labor Statistics, about one-third of minimum wage earners are teenagers and another 10 to 20 percent are young adults. In addition, about half of minimum wage earners are employed part-time, and many are single and live in a home with a relative as the head of the household.

Any raise in the minimum wage will cost businesses an amount far exceeding the amount specified by law because it also increases unemployment insurance premiums, workers' compensation premiums, Social Security and disability benefit costs, and pushes up all other wages. These costs are not just absorbed by the affected businesses. In the end, they cost jobs.

For example, the National Restaurant Association surveyed its membership's reaction to a 1980 minimum wage increase. More than 70 percent had reduced employee work hours, 48 percent laid off workers, and 28 percent had added labor-saving equipment. In addition, more than 90 percent raised prices. This is especially relevant because the food industry is the largest employer of minimum wage earners.

A better solution would be to offer incentives for apprenticeship programs to help give workers the skills they need to move out of the minimum wage category. This concept is supported by President Clinton, but not necessarily as a substitute for raising the minimum wage.

Labor Law Reform

With the new administration will come a push by big labor and its friends in Congress to undertake a significant reform of the nation's labor laws, specifically to rewrite the National Labor Relations Act. This was last undertaken during the Carter administration.

While major restructuring of the nation's labor laws will probably not be led by the White House, it will find little opposition there. In fact, President Clinton has already stated support for one of its goals: striker replacement. What concerns small businesses about any revision in the labor laws is the change in the balance between unions and management which will likely result.

Big labor is lining up support in Congress to push for labor law reform. Reforms likely to be considered when-rewriting the National Labor Relations Act (NLRA) are: a broader definition of "unfair labor practice," the broadening of unions' right to organize and the granting of more rights to strike for union recognition.

Parts of these reforms were considered in the 102nd Congress, and will likely appear again. They include several items that affect small businesses directly.

Striker Replacement

In 1938, the U.S. Supreme Court ruled the National Labor Relations Act does not prevent employers from hiring replacement workers for employees who have walked off the job in an economic strike (a strike over issues such as pay, hours and benefits). However, after a settlement, the striking workers have the right to jobs that replacement workers leave. During several economic labor disputes in the 1980s, employers exercised their rights under the NLRA to permanently replace striking workers in order to continue operations.

In 1992, big labor declared preventing employers from permanently replacing striking workers to be their number one priority. Legislation introduced in the 102nd Congress would have amended the NLRA to make it an unfair labor practice to permanently replace workers during a strike or to give employment preference to workers who cross picket lines. The legislation passed the House, but died in the Senate.

In his campaign outline, *Putting People First*, Bill Clinton pledged to sign legislation that would ban the permanent replacement of striking workers. This legislation, likely to be reintroduced early in the 103rd Congress, could shape up to be big labor's best organizing tool in decades. As originally written, the defeated legislation would have prevented any employer from replacing not only workers of a recognized union, but also non-union workers. This could have opened up small businesses to union organizing.

Right-To-Work

As governor of Arkansas, Bill Clinton presided over a right-to-work state. Like other states with right-to-work laws, Arkansas benefits from its pro-business environment as new businesses locate there and existing businesses expand operations. But in one of the most puzzling positions in the campaign, candidate Clinton said he would sign legislation to override a state's ability to have right-to-work laws if Congress passed such a bill.

Right-to-work laws are state laws which prevent membership or non-membership in a labor union from being a condition for employing an individual. Twenty states have explicit right-to-work laws, while more than 30 states have right-to-work protections for at least some public employees. In addition, federal employees are protected by right-to-work provisions.

Right-to-work laws have been protected by federal statute since 1947 by Section 14b of the Taft-Hartley amendments to the National Labor Relations Act. No concerted action was taken to change them until 1965 when a group backed by then-President Lyndon Johnson sought repeal of Section 14b. The effort failed, as have all efforts since then to repeal right-to-work provisions, despite the well-financed lobbying by organized labor.

In the campaign book, *Putting People First*, President Clinton and Vice President Gore stated, "we support the repeal of Section 14b of the Taft-Hartley Act to create a level playing field between labor and management."

Child Labor

Young people benefit from jobs by gaining experience

Labor and the Workplace

and developing confidence, self-discipline and an understanding of the free enterprise system. Small businesses hire many young people and as a result, enable them to gain experience through a summer job or to contribute to the family's income by becoming an active member of the work force. However, teenagers need protection from potentially harmful job situations.

Child labor is regulated at both the state and federal level. At the federal level, children are protected under the Fair Labor Standards Act of 1938 and numerous amendments and revisions since. Federal law limits the number of hours teenagers under 16 years of age can work. Teenagers under 18 are prohibited from certain occupations, such as manufacturing and mining. Teenagers are also banned from using certain heavy equipment. And, in general, employment of children under 14 is prohibited. Violations can result in civil penalties and for repeat offenders, imprisonment.

State child labor laws vary and are more specific regarding local industries, but in general, are more restrictive than federal laws.

Further restrictions on child labor and stiffer penalties for infractions came to the forefront of political debate in late 1990 after then-Secretary of Labor Elizabeth Dole undertook a major government investigation of more than 9,500 businesses. In what was called "Operation Child Watch," the government found 40,000 violations. That same year, the maximum civil penalty for non-serious violations of child labor laws was increased to $10,000 per violation, and for willful violations, it went up to $100,000 each, a ten-fold increase from previous maximums.

President Clinton has not stated any specific legislative initiatives on child labor laws. However, there is a myriad of possible Hill-backed legislation, including further restrictions on the hours a child can work, prohibitions to additional industries, more extensive machine guidelines, increases in penalties for violations and outright child labor bans.

The 102nd Congress considered legislation that would have created vague new categories of child labor violations — some resulting in criminal penalties, additional layers of bureaucracy through federal work permits and posting in schools the names of child labor law violators.

Requiring a federal work permit to employ a teenager is bad for both small business and the teenager. This government mandate would create an entire bureaucracy wasting taxpayer money and increasing the cost of employing teenagers. Work permits are already required in 38 states. But a permit at the federal level would create yet another layer of paperwork for the small business owner. Nevertheless, the legislation will likely be reintroduced in some form.

Another bureaucracy-building proposal that has been considered in the past would require the distribution of names of businesses which have violated child labor laws to the local schools, where the names would be posted. And, the National Education Association has proposed requiring employers to get written permission from school principals before hiring young people.

While teenagers need protection in the workplace and child labor restrictions are politically popular, excessive regulation can effectively eliminate job opportunities for all young people. The additional regulations and paperwork, along with the increasing civil and criminal liabilities could make it too expensive and too risky to hire young people anymore, which is bad for small business, but worse for the teenagers who need a job and who want to work.

Family Leave

One of the first pieces of workplace legislation likely to be considered by Congress and President Clinton will be a bill regarding family leave. A family leave mandate was passed in the 102nd Congress. It was vetoed by former President Bush, and his veto was sustained in the House. As a candidate, Bill Clinton pledged to sign a family leave bill. Indeed, he made it a constant point in his stump speeches.

Proponents of family leave legislation argue that employees want and need it, that it will help women in the work force and that it will be inexpensive for businesses to provide.

Not one of these claims is true. According to numerous surveys, family leave ranks near the bottom of benefits employees want; it will reduce employment opportunities for women; and it significantly increases the cost of doing business. It has big supporters in Congress because it sounds like good politics.

The legislation vetoed by former President Bush, the Family and Medical Leave Act of 1991, would have required businesses to grant up to 12 weeks of unpaid leave for the birth, adoption, foster care of a child or in case of the illness of a child, spouse, parent or oneself. Small businesses with 50 or fewer employees were exempted from the mandate.

However, with a family leave supporter in the White House, many expect a move to lower or eliminate the exemption over time. This has created concern, and with good reason. One of family leave's strongest proponents, Rep. Pat Schroeder (D-Colo.), said that an "even stronger" bill would be introduced in 1993. One of the most likely strengthening measures would be to lower or eliminate the small business exemption. Sen. Edward Kennedy (D-Mass.) has said, "I believe once established, (mandated leave) legislation will be expanded over the years."

A small business atmosphere fosters negotiated benefits packages that take into account the individual needs of each employee. A government mandate for an inflexible, impersonal, one-size-fits-all benefit plan ignores the needs of an individual employee. Surveys have shown that a majority of Americans prefer to see employers and employees decide on a package that best fits individual needs instead of trying to fit into a single government mandated benefit package.

A mandate also interjects government into and disrupts the natural employer-employee relationship. As a small business grows, so too do the benefits offered to an employee. Traditionally, the first benefit is vacation and sick leave. As the business prospers, employers consult with employees and expand the benefit package to include such things as health insurance, dental insurance, life insurance or paid prescription drugs.

A government mandate disrupts this relationship and demands that the first benefit offered be mandated leave, which may or may not be in the interests of employees. Numerous studies show that making parental leave the most important employer-provided benefit is out of step with the desire of the employees:

• A 1991 study by Penn-Shoen/Concerned Alliance of Responsible Employers found that 89 percent of employees prefer to have benefits negotiated between employer and employee, not imposed through a federal mandate.

• In a 1990 Gallup/Employee Benefit Research Institute poll, only 1 percent of those polled considered parental leave as the most important employer-provided benefit, while 16 percent named it as the least important.

• A 1990 ABC News/Washington Post poll asked respondents to rank four items in order of importance – raising the minimum wage, providing parental leave, making affordable day care available, and taking stronger action to clean the nation's water and air. Parental leave was ranked last, cited by only 3 percent of those polled.

If family leave must be the first benefit offered, the others, which are much more important to employees, will suffer. The cost of the mandate will be paid by employees through cuts in other benefits, such as salary increases and health insurance coverage. When economically possible, companies already offer family leave. A 1991 Gallup/NFIB survey showed that 93 percent of small businesses offered some form of family leave, usually negotiated between employers and employees.

A major reason proponents of mandated family leave give for the legislation is to help women stay in the work force. However, the mandate would have the opposite effect. Unintentionally, it would encourage employers to discriminate against women. Faced with a mandated leave, a business owner choosing between two equally qualified candidates – one male and one female – will select the male for the simple reason that many businesses cannot afford to have employees out for two-and-a-half months.

Proponents claim the only employer cost of family leave will be in the form of health insurance for the person on leave. However, there are significant other costs, including those related to finding, hiring and training a temporary worker. In 35 states, employers must pay unemployment compensation when a temporary worker leaves. Each claim raises the company's unemployment compensation insurance premium. As costs mount, business owners must make choices about jobs and benefits. A struggling business owner would rather cut benefits than jobs. But if family leave is mandated, businesses may be forced to cut jobs.

Davis-Bacon

The Davis-Bacon Act, enacted in 1931, requires business owners who enter into contracts with the federal government, to pay "prevailing wages," usually the union scale of the nearest metropolitan area, to the various classes of laborers working under those contracts. The legislation's effect of equalizing the wages of competing firms was originally designed to help small local firms compete with large corporations on large government contracts. In an effort to include only large projects, it was written (in 1931) to cover projects exceeding $2,000. These outdated regulations have the opposite effect of the legislation's original intention.

Today the $2,000 threshold covers virtually every contract granted, including construction, alteration or repair of public buildings and public works, and painting or decorating. A positive change to Davis-Bacon would be an increase in the outdated contract thresholds, a move that would limit the law to the large contracts for which it was originally intended. This would be positive for small businesses because smaller contracts would no longer require the mountain of Davis-Bacon paperwork, allowing the very small contractor to compete for government projects, many for the first time. In addition, it would save money.

While the Davis-Bacon regulations were originally designed to help small, local firms compete for government contracts, they have just the opposite effect today. By equalizing the labor costs, the regulations take away the advantage such firms have over their larger counterparts – that of price. In addition, by taking price out of the equation, Davis-Bacon projects cost the taxpayer more money.

During the 102nd Congress, several changes to Davis-Bacon were considered, all of which are likely to reappear. One change overwhelmingly opposed by small business would expand Davis-Bacon to material suppliers, manufacturers, independent contractors and employers operating in leased facilities. This is an effort by organized labor to get big, unionized contractors involved in every aspect of government projects. Expansion of Davis-Bacon into other areas of construction would be very harmful to small business because it would raise the costs of doing business and would make it more difficult for small businesses to compete with larger contractors.

Clinton has made no statements on specific legislation considered in past Congresses or likely to appear in the future. He has said only that he supports enforcement of the prevailing wage protections provided by the act.

Comprehensive Reform of the Occupational Health and Safety Administration

Organized labor has been pushing for dramatic changes to current laws governing the Occupational Safety and Health Administration (OSHA) for some time. An indication of the kinds of burdens they want to put on all businesses was seen in legislation considered by the 102nd Congress. As the first comprehensive OSHA reform legislation in 20 years, it contained some 50 basic provisions. Fortunately for small business, that legislation was defeated.

The OSHA reform legislation was drafted by and lobbied for by organized labor and is proclaimed to be one of its top 10 issues. However, anticipating a friendlier atmosphere in 1993, labor did not push with the full force of its muscle in 1992. President Clinton said little specifically in the campaign about OSHA reform except for a pledge to fully enforce OSHA guidelines. However, the coalition that elected him will push hard for increased regulation of and involvement in the workplace. If this push succeeds, it would radically change OSHA guidelines in ways that would be especially harmful to small business.

The OSHA reform bill's "reforms" would change the structure of management-employee relations through the creation of safety committees, expand criminal penalties for employers and increase paperwork through requiring written safety plans.

Worker Safety Committees

Under the OSHA reform legislation, all businesses with 11 or more employees must create worker safety committees made up of employee and management representatives. These committees would be required to conduct meetings and inspections every three months. They would have the right to review employee safety records. If enacted, these committees will cost businesses thousands of dollars in unproductive time and compliance with the associated paperwork, draining precious resources needed to remain competitive.

Richard Pouliot, president of Applied Specialties, Inc., a Beltsville, Maryland, company specializing in wholesale radio frequency components and cable assemblies, believes the proposed legislation would significantly increase the cost of doing business.

Pouliot, whose business has 14 full-time and two part-time employees, testified before the House Small Business Committee, Subcommittee on Regulation, Business Opportunities, and Energy in April of 1992:

> *"The cost of one of our managers participating in such a committee would be about $20 an hour while a non-management individual would cost about $10 an hour. With taxes and benefits, the estimated direct cost without other employees participating is approximately $36 an hour. I estimate my direct costs from safety and health committees to be somewhere around $3,600 the first year and $1,000 each year thereafter. If this cost*

could be offset by reductions in workmen's compensation, I would be happy. But, I think mandated safety committees are not cost effective for small business. And, not even Congress can legislate a cooperative attitude."

In addition, the committees may conflict with provisions of the Taft-Hartley Labor-Management Relations Act and with terms of previously negotiated labor contracts at certain businesses.

Big labor will push hard for the creation of worker safety committees. Not only do they fundamentally alter the nature of management-labor relations, they also create an environment ripe for union organization.

In one version of the OSHA reform bill, union organizing through the committees was prohibited. But even with the prohibition, the structure of the committee facilitates union organization. In addition, some believe these committees may be considered bargaining units by the judicial system. If this is the case, the government would have created a *de facto* union in every business with more than 11 employees.

Expansion of Criminal Penalties

Under current law, if an employee is killed on the job and the accident is determined to be the fault of the employer, the employer may be criminally liable. Under the OSHA reform bill, the employer may be criminally liable if an employee suffers "serious bodily injury" resulting from a "willful violation" of regulations. While the expansion of penalties is bad enough, the vague terms could open the floodgates of lawsuits on injuries that OSHA was never meant to cover. Each such lawsuit, with or without merit, could cost small business owners tens of thousands of dollars to fight, win or lose.

In his testimony before Congress, Pouliot stated his belief that the proposed legislation is too vague and that the criminal penalties promote fear of and an adversarial relationship with OSHA:

"Definitions for 'serious bodily injury' and 'willful violations' are so vague and difficult to understand that if an accident were to occur in my business, I would probably only be able to determine their meaning in court. The fear of possible criminal action would keep me from seeking OSHA assistance after even a minor accident occurs. The result will be that I will not be able to work with OSHA and this will hurt workplace safety."

A Written Safety and Health Program

The OSHA reform bill requires all businesses to create a written safety and health program. The document demanded by the legislation is very detailed, requiring extensive explanations of methods and procedures for identifying safety and health hazards as well as procedures for providing safety and health training. In addition, no business is exempt. Proponents of the health and safety program claim that shifting this responsibility to employers would help stretch OSHA's budget. However, they fail to recognize the enormous financial burden this would put on small businesses.

While the document may be easily created by larger businesses with experience in dealing with OSHA, it will be a paperwork nightmare for small business owners who have never dealt with OSHA before. The cost of administering the completion of these plans will be enormous.

In his testimony before Congress, Pouliot, (mentioned above) told about his successful individualized training program at Applied Specialties, Inc.:

"Our business provides safety through an informal management procedure which saves costs while providing training in safety to our employees. I personally take each employee through our safety manual. This method works best for our business and has resulted in a healthy atmosphere in which very few of our long-term employees use sick leave. The formalized actions required by (the proposed legislation) are not that tailored to our small business. They will require more time, will cost more money, and not result in increased safety."

9

Reducing the Crushing Weight of Government Regulation and Paperwork

Americans with Disabilities Act
Clean Air Act Amendments
Paperwork Reduction Act, Third Party Disclosure
The Regulatory Flexibility Act

For a small business owner, next to death and taxes, government-imposed regulation is the greatest certainty. It is also the most direct and consistent link that American businesses have to their federal government. Regulations are the door through which the government intrudes on the operations of small businesses on a daily, even hourly basis.

Regulations mean paperwork, stacks of it, up to a foot thick, just to start some types of businesses, according to one study. Paperwork means time lost from business operations — and time is money. And when a small business loses money, the community loses jobs.

Entrepreneurs are endowed with an independent spirit. So there is little wonder why small business owners feel that government involvement in their lives, on any level, is an imposition. They view with disdain the inefficient way government traditionally operates. And then, this inefficient body mandates how a small business must be run. It is a frustrating fact of life for independent business owners in America.

Small business owners agree with the laudable goals of laws like the Americans with Disabilities Act, the Pollution Prevention Act, the Clean Air Act, and the Nutrition Labeling and Education Act, to name only a few. But with the passage of each such law, a bureaucracy of regulations and regulation enforcers springs forth; growing, ever growing, finding new ways to justify its existence. Too often the justification seems to pile on paperwork for the small business owner.

The questions concerning regulations and paperwork are, simply, questions of economics. What is the economic burden borne by businesses as a result of these laws? And is the burden fairly distributed among all citizens? Is there any one group paying a greater price? Typically, the result of government regulation is that certain special interest groups prosper, while the overall strength of the economy suffers.

Dramatic Increase of Regulation

By any measure, the amount of government regulation on small business has increased dramatically over the last several years. Certainly the number of government regulators on the federal payroll is a good indication. That number has increased since 1989 by 16,400 persons to a 1992 total — and an all-time high — of 122,400. The growth is even more dramatic when measured against the figures of 1970, when the number of regulators was 71,233.

An abundance of evidence exists illustrating the recent astounding growth of government regulation:

- The United States spent 22 percent more on regulatory activities in 1991 than it did in 1980.

- In 1988, government "regulations in development" numbered 4,000; the count is now up to 4,900 (not including existing government regulations).

- Since 1989, the federal government has issued more than 5,000 new rules.

- The period from 1988 to 1991 saw the largest expansion in federal regulations since the 1970s.

- In 1970, the government's total regulatory administrative costs equaled $3.4 billion. In 1991, it was up to $9.1 billion.

- Since 1986, 10 of the most burdensome and costly regulatory measures for businesses were passed, including in 1990 and 1991 alone, the Clean Air Act Amendments, the Nutrition Labeling and Education Act, the Americans with Disabilities Act and the Civil Rights Act.

The following chart prepared by the Congressional Joint Economic Committee further illustrates the recent astounding growth of government regulatory burdens on small business:

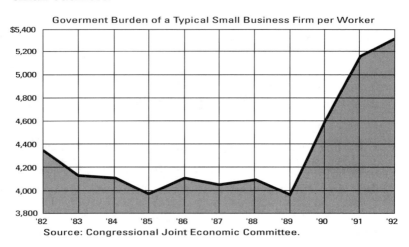
Source: Congressional Joint Economic Committee.

As can be expected, such an explosion in regulatory activity can show up on the bottom lines of small businesses, as this chart shows:

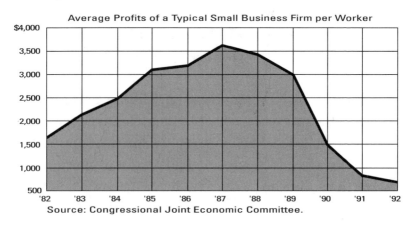
Source: Congressional Joint Economic Committee.

Disproportional Burden for Small Business

The Small Business Administration has reported the proportional cost of regulation per employee is three times higher for smaller businesses than for larger businesses. Small business owners know all too well how Uncle Sam's attempt to standardize regulations — that is, issue "one size fits all" mandates — can produce "diseconomies of scale" in regulatory compliance. Because these burdens hit smaller firms much harder, the regulations, in effect, create unintended barriers to new businesses entering the market, inhibiting the development of new products and reducing competition.

Granted, being subjected to government rules is a necessity of doing business. However, the recent number of new and expanded regulations is hitting small business owners like machine gun fire. This regulatory load is consuming many small businesses due to the enormous amounts of time owners must spend ensuring eligibility and compliance, rather than running the business. Overregulation absorbs capital, time and human resources that could and should be used to increase productivity, stimulate innovation and create jobs.

Owners of small businesses can tell you that government regulation is often surprisingly deceptive. The effect of regulation on their business — and on the economy as a whole — can be every bit as destructive as the imposition of taxes. Taxes may be a more overt, more scrutinized form of government involvement, but government regulation is a hidden burden that small business finds difficult to defend against and harder and harder to afford.

Regulations Endangering the Small Business Environment

In a June 1992 article in the *Wall Street Journal*, several interviews illustrate how legislators' good intentions concerning environmental laws have gone awry and have become counterproductive for businesses and the economy as a whole:

- *Richard Cox Jr., president of Camden Tanning Corporation in Camden, Maine, says the latest puzzles are the rules governing hazardous-waste disposal. "Where does it go?" he wonders. "How much do we send in? We're not engineers, so we try and do the best we can. You can't fight 'em." Mr. Cox says his company, which tans leather on contract for manufacturers, spends about one-third of its fixed overhead on environmental items. "Our biggest problem is the paperwork. If they require a study, we have to hire somebody. That could be $30,000."*

- *Bo Brasfield, co-owner of B&M Tractor Parts Inc. in Taylor, Texas, says complex new rules on disposing of tires and waste oil are counterproductive. "You have less liability if you go out in the middle of the night and dump it in a ditch. They've created a monster," he says. In the past three years, Mr. Brasfield says he has spent* *about 25 percent of his working hours, and B&M has spent $68,000, or about 3 percent of sales, to comply with environmental rules. "That doesn't leave you just a whole lot."*

The burden is already topping $109 billion in annual environmental regulation costs, according to a study conducted by the Rochester Institute of Technology. The same study estimates total regulatory costs to the economy between $430 billion and $562 billion per year. The EPA's own estimate of environmental regulatory compliance (prior to the enactment of the Clean Air Act in 1991) was $86 billion in 1988.

Large corporations generally are able to comply with these environmental regulations far easier than small businesses. Large corporations can draw from experts on staff to negotiate the maze of regulatory paperwork, while small companies often must hire additional clerical help and purchase expensive record-keeping equipment just to keep up.

In fact, an EPA study analyzed the effect of 85 of its "major" regulations since 1987 in terms of costs for compliance. The study, compiled by category, revealed: dry cleaning compliance costs were up to $12,700; interstate trucking, up to $6,765; farm supply, up to $16,675; pesticide formulation and packaging, up to $18,240; and electroplating, up to $20,110. A chilling fact revealed in the study was that in the majority of these industries, the costs to comply with environmental regulations exceeded the average annual net profits for those companies.

The Regulatory Results of the Americans with Disabilities Act and the Clean Air Act

No one disagrees that disabled people deserve access to the same buildings, parks, museums, elevators and all the public places as those without physical and other challenges. Likewise, no one disagrees that cleaner air would improve the quality of life for every American. Unfortunately, the Clean Air Act amendments and the Americans with Disabilities Act, both passed in 1990, are two of the largest hidden tax burdens to hit small business owners in recent times, perhaps ever.

A February 1992 *Wall Street Journal* article concluded that Congress and the Bush administration grossly underestimated the cost to comply with both these burdensome acts, and that vague wording of the legislation had only made the problem worse. The article reported: "The official estimate for complying with the Clean Air Act was put at roughly $25 billion per year. Nongovernmental estimates of the cost of complying with the act range as high as $100 billion per year."

The Americans with Disabilities Act was originally estimated to cost $2 billion per year for compliance. The *Wall Street Journal* estimates that compliance for office space alone could reach $45 billion. "The cost of compliance appears to be close to $5 per square foot. There are an estimated 150,000 square feet in an average office building. This places the cost of compliance at almost $1 million per building. There are an estimated nine billion square feet of office space in the nation, bringing the total compliance cost nationwide to $45 billion. And that's just for office space."

"The American Hospital Association ... estimates that its members will have to spend $20 billion to bring hospitals into compliance," according to the article. That puts the total at $65 billion, not counting the cost of compliance for public transportation, restaurants and other public facilities.

These acts, passed in 1990, are illustrations of the kinds of legislation that can jeopardize the existence of a small business, because smaller businesses are affected in disproportionately larger measure than larger corporations.

President Clinton and Government Regulation

With the election of Bill Clinton to the White House, the question of what will happen to the regulatory burden on business and, more specifically, on small business is an important concern. Nothing less than our nation's productivity and competitiveness is riding on the answer to this question.

As America seems more and more to be a nation of paper pushers instead of producers, the level of frustration on the part of small business owners is rising. Many believe the obstacles have become too great, as one business owner recently said, "Why should I even bother to try to hang on to this business? Every time I turn around the government is trying to drive me out of it. I'm tired of it. It just isn't worth the trouble anymore."

The problem may be reaching a crisis level, as most small business experts believe government regulation under President Clinton will only increase, as it has under every president before him.

However, that is not necessarily a reflection of the policies Clinton intends to back. Regulatory burdens never seem to decrease, regardless of who is president. If there are new laws, there is more paperwork.

Even if enlightened policy makers could find a way to slow the increase, there would still be an increase. According to a November 1992 report, *Derailing the Small Business Job Express*, prepared by the Congressional Joint Economic Committee, the increasing use of mandates by Congress to correct social problems results in the explosive growth of job threatening regulation. This trend, the report states, is the reason businesses in 1992 faced "a climate in which they were burdened with about $130 billion of costs beyond those of 1990."

The report cautions that "mandates and regulations impose burdens that represent 'hidden' taxes in the American economy. This gives the effect of expanding government programs without appearing to increase the size of government."

For these reasons, small business owners strive to curb government regulation. It is in order to protect their American heritage — the work ethic that leads to the American dream — that determined, honest labor will yield success.

What Small Businesses Can Do

As with any new president, the arrival of Bill Clinton in Washington means more regulatory burdens as Congress enacts more and more legislation to fulfill his political agenda. However, government agencies under President Clinton's direction, together with the Congress, must recognize the cumulative effect of the vast array of regulation heaped on small business.

They must especially note how the rule-making process takes a harmful "one size fits all" approach.

Federal agencies and Congress must review the regulatory process while considering the size and capabilities of small firms and the disproportionate burden that excessive regulation imposes on the most vital job creating facet of our economy.

To this end, there are specific legislative proposals that will come before the Congress and the president which small business owners will continue to support. They are:

Paperwork Reduction Act — Third Party Disclosure

The Heritage Foundation has reported that reviewing and filling out tax paperwork *alone* takes the equivalent of nearly three million full-time workers each year. Based on this, the foundation estimates that every federal program actually costs the country 65 percent more than was previously thought. For example, the Davis-Bacon Act, which is more than 50 years old, requires any company which obtains a federal government construction or services contract to pay union scale wages.

According to the U.S. Labor Department, construction firms must file some 11 million weekly payroll reports to comply. The price tag: 5.5 million hours of paperwork handling, costing $100 million a year. The result: fewer small businesses willing to pursue federal contracts, with the loss of competition taking its toll on the federal government and, ultimately, taxpayers.

The cost of excessive paperwork doesn't hit just the construction industry. The Small Business Administration estimates that business owners from all sectors spent 1 billion hours filling out government paperwork in 1988 alone, at a cost of $100 billion. To help stem the tide, the Paperwork Reduction Act was enacted in 1980 to eliminate unnecessary and duplicate paperwork. The law created a department within the Office of Management and Budget (OMB) to review and approve all government-imposed paperwork requests.

Simply telling federal agencies to curb the amount of paperwork they generate has proven ineffective. Employees of federal agencies naturally want to perpetuate their jobs and thus are not inclined to heed requests to scale back their agency's regulatory purpose. The Paperwork Reduction Act is a tool small businesses can use to fight the burdens of overregulation.

A recent Supreme Court decision undermined the intent of the Paperwork Reduction Act when it ruled that paperwork requested by government agencies which must be "posted," or simply kept in the business, does not have to be reviewed by the paperwork reduction office. In other words, any paperwork that a business must post for employees, or keep in the business's files, such as **OSHA** forms, W-2 forms, immigration forms, is no longer covered under the Paperwork Reduction Act. This ruling's effect has been to exempt approximately one-third of all government paperwork from any kind of review.

This allows the government to require virtually anything they desire without a review process for small businesses to assess the regulation's burden. If it is too burdensome, if the form is too complicated, if anything doesn't work, small business will have no recourse.

While President Clinton has not yet committed to a position on this legislation, he has said he is committed to helping ease the burden of regulation on business. Small business owners are fighting to restore third party disclosures to coverage under the Paperwork Reduction Act and restore the original intent of the legislation.

Regulatory Flexibility and Judicial Review

The Regulatory Flexibility Act is another of the limited tools available to protect small business from the impact of government regulation.

Passed in 1980, this act is designed to ensure that federal agencies take into account the potential economic impact of government regulations on small entities including small towns, not-for-profit operations, and small businesses. The Small Business Administration is charged with monitoring the law.

However, several weaknesses and loopholes in the statute prevent it from being fully effective with regard to small business.

The one agency that affects *all* businesses, the Internal Revenue Service, exempted itself from the law despite Congress' undisputed intent to include all agencies within the law's scope. Similarly, the Department of Defense often exempts itself from the law, claiming national security warrants it. This is especially unfortunate considering how small businesses could benefit from restrictions on the department's cumbersome purchasing practices and extensive paperwork requirements.

The good news for small business is that, as a candidate, President Clinton promised to enforce the Regulatory Flexibility Act's provisions for reducing the regulatory burdens on small business. In addition, he has said he will develop regulatory short forms for use by small businesses, much like the short forms used for federal taxes.

The Challenge to Clinton

While regulation is a "necessary evil" of a modern political and economic system, saddling small businesses with a disproportionate share of the regulatory burden will always be damaging to the nation's economy.

Small business advocates will look for President Clinton and his administration to move away from mandates and overregulation, which understand no differentiation between small businesses and large corporations, toward more flexible options such as economic incentives to encourage businesses to solve problems in society.

10

Protecting the Environment, Protecting Small Business

Property Rights
Just Compensation
RCRA (Solid Waste Disposal)
Community Right to Know More

A New Jersey restaurant owner planning to expand his business purchased land across a small creek adjacent to his lot. It wasn't until he requested a building permit that he was told his property could not be developed. It had been classified as a wetland even though there was no evidence of any continual saturation.

Not only was the restaurant owner not able to expand, he was stuck with land he cannot use or sell, but on which he must still pay taxes based on its original value. This nightmare may force him to lay off employees or close.

When it comes to environmental issues, most agree the planet needs protecting. What few people realize is that the best intentions rarely translate into good regulations.

"Good regulations?" A contradiction in terms for most small business owners, and for good reason: regulatory interference in nature, as in business, just doesn't work.

Because they work, live and are active in their communities, small business owners are often pioneers in community-based recycling and conservation efforts. However, Congress' efforts on behalf of the environment have not helped them in this fight.

Instead, legislation likely to come before the 103rd Congress could strangle small business with even more "green tape," stringent environmental regulations that jack up capital and administrative costs associated with environmental regulations. The result: Small businesses will be hit hardest at a time when they should be given every break to create jobs.

New environmental legislation will likely come to the fore early in the Clinton administration. There is little doubt that Vice President Gore will lobby for stronger environmental programs. When he announced his running mate, President Clinton said Gore would be his top advisor on environmental issues.

Small business owners should pay close attention to new environmental legislation, which could affect many businesses previously untouched by regulation. This legislation includes reauthorization of the Endangered Species Act (ESA), wetlands reform, reauthorization of the Resource Conservation and Recovery Act (RCRA), and the Community Right to Know More provision of RCRA.

Property Rights

No other example better illustrates the importance of

the conflict between environmental regulations and jobs than that of the infamous Northern Spotted Owl. The controversy also demonstrates the power of small business to command attention when injustice occurs. At the heart of the issue is the basic American right to private property. In the Pacific Northwest, hundreds of farmers and small business owners have been denied economic use of their land because of overprotective, impractical regulations.

Almost 7 million acres spanning three states have been designated as critical habitat for the Spotted Owl. Between 50,000 to 100,000 jobs are estimated to have been lost – and not just in the timber industry. The loss of a major employment base threatens a host of support businesses and their employees: grocery stores, restaurants, builders, plumbers, gas stations and mechanics.

The root of the problem lies in the misguided ESA, which was up for reauthorization during the 102nd Congress. Having failed to pass then, it will likely resurface in the 103rd. Similar legislation regarding reform of wetlands policy is affecting small business owners as well.

The Endangered Species Act (ESA)

Reauthorization of the ESA should not be an adversarial issue between environmentalists and small business. No one advocates the wanton extinction of any species. Many who have studied the problem, however, agree that the ESA is a misdirected law. It is a law of absolutes that ignores its own impact and offers no means of redress.

The act has no flexibility to allow it to adapt to the myriad environmental conditions it was set up to assist.

As a result, this "pit bull" law fails to accomplish its good intentions. If the ESA is to be effective and deserving of support, it should not be reauthorized in its present form. Small business owners should press legislators to support amendments to bring this act under control.

Where It Went Wrong

The ESA began as an exercise in futility. More than 1,200 species and subspecies were originally listed as endangered or threatened, 676 of them in the United States. Another 3,500 are waiting to be added to the list. The Council on Environmental Quality has noted that the Natural Heritage data base reported as many as 9,000 domestic species at risk. The ESA has clearly bitten off more than it can chew. It is arguable that the law too often tries to protect species that would become extinct from the forces of natural selection anyway, thereby impeding, rather than serving, nature.

A troubling trend is the listing of species that are not few in number or confined to a few specific sites. These creatures, such as the Northern Spotted Owl, Snake River Sockeye Salmon and Desert Tortoise, have large populations across multi-state regions. Protecting them isn't a case of stopping one shopping center or dam – it has the potential to disrupt the economies of entire regions.

In the case of the Spotted Owl, the University of Oregon

has estimated that local taxes would have to increase 1,000 percent in five Oregon counties and by hundreds of percent in several others to replace the revenue lost from their statutory share of federal timber sale receipts.

The courts do not even require evidence of real injury to an individual member of a listed species to establish that a landowner is guilty of illegally harming it. In a federal suit in Hawaii, the court ruled that harm may be proved by statistics alone – statistics not related to the landowner's property but to the entire territory the species occupies.

As a result, many reasonable and productive uses of property by its rightful owners — such as clearing brush, building homes and protecting livestock from predators — are being substantially curtailed or blocked by the ESA. Landowners have received no just compensation from the government for their loss. Property values have been depressed or destroyed in cavalier disregard of the Constitutional protection of property rights.

Relief Measures Not Working

The ESA was amended in 1978 and 1982 to provide two processes for landowners seeking relief. Unfortunately, exorbitant costs, lengthy delays and insurmountable procedural barriers have made these processes virtually impossible for small business. The 1982 amendment allows private landowners to submit "habitat conservation plans" to the Fish and Wildlife Service in the hope of receiving "incidental take permits." In the decade since, only a dozen or so such permits have been granted after years of negotiations and thousands of dollars in expenses.

Just Compensation

Whenever a discussion of the property rights of private business owners begins, the term "just compensation" is likely to arise. It is, after all, a Constitutional guarantee – unless it concerns wetlands, where the Constitution doesn't seem to apply. The U.S. Fish and Wildlife Service or the Army Corps of Engineers can simply declare an area a wetland and, suddenly, its economic use ends.

No one will disagree that wetlands preservation is a worthy goal. Wetlands play a vital role in filtering water, preventing soil erosion, replenishing the ozone, and providing habitat for a variety of animal life. But when a farmer is told he may no longer use his land because a roadside ditch along his property held water for two weeks after heavy rains, something is wrong. Such is the broad and misapplied definition of wetlands.

What Went Wrong

The problem with wetlands reform intensified in 1989 when the Army Corps of Engineers in conjunction with the Fish and Wildlife Service began using a new wetlands delineation manual. This broadened the definition of a wetland to the extent that, technically, property may be declared a wetland for something as small as a ditch that sometimes contains water. Since then, the number of regulated wetlands has tripled, with no compensation for the owners who lost the use and value of their property. The Constitution guarantees that when property is seized, for example, to build a highway, the owner should receive fair and just compensation for the loss. Yet, under the current regulatory system, these basic rights are being denied by an unelected bureaucracy of federal agencies.

Legislation That Can Help

The 102nd Congress failed to act on an important bill, the Comprehensive Wetlands Conservation and Management Act, that could have provided the consistent, structured approach the present system needs. The legislation should be reintroduced during the 103rd session. Understanding that all wetlands are not created equal, the bill classified wetlands under three categories. Only the environmentally "most valuable wetlands," such as swamps, bogs and marshes, make the regulatory cut, and restrictions on others are eased. The bill also sets up parameters based on value for compensation.

Environmentalists should welcome this reform. It will allow regulatory agencies to focus their efforts on the most important wetland areas. It may also serve to deflect the criticism generated from those who have been hurt economically by the current unwieldy system.

The Resource Conservation and Recovery Act (RCRA)

Small business owners justly complain that environmental laws are often too technical and burdensome. Although they want to help clean up the environment, they cannot afford the lawyers, permit specialists or staff engineers to decipher regulations, especially in the case of the Resource Conservation and Recovery Act (RCRA). The act was not reauthorized in the 102nd Congress, but will likely be reconsidered during the 103rd Congress.

Just as the Clean Air Act was the major environmental effort for the 101st Congress, reauthorization of RCRA was the focus of the 102nd. RCRA is the nation's primary solid and hazardous waste law. It regulates the disposal of municipal solid waste – the trash collected by cities from homes and businesses. The bill's authorization expired in 1988, but has continued at original funding levels since.

The reauthorization legislation and its accompanying amendments proposed numerous changes that would impose costly, long-range regulatory burdens on a variety of small businesses. Legislation expected to be reintroduced in the 103rd Congress will likely address such areas as solid waste management, industrial waste, recycling and Community Right to Know More provisions.

Solid Waste Management

One amendment to RCRA sought to impose a new permitting process for businesses engaged in treating or disposing of municipal solid waste. Generally, this provision would affect only waste-related businesses, but one exception was made for businesses that collect recyclable items to sell to a recycler. Technically, this could mean any small business collecting recyclable trash, such as a grocery store or dry cleaner, could face permitting. Supporters insisted that was not the bill's intent, but there should be a clearer distinction between waste management facilities and businesses that collect items to be recycled.

Industrial Waste

RCRA's industrial waste provisions proposed a regulatory system for companies that generate, store or dispose of industrial waste, such as scrap. A small quantity exception was made for businesses that generate less than 1,000 kilograms (2,200 pounds) per month of industrial waste.

But the draft did not include a similar exception for owners of waste management facilities that store or dispose of small amounts of industrial waste or manage such waste for only limited periods of time. Thus, a business such as an auto repair shop that generates only a small amount of waste, such as used oil, and temporarily stores it on-site before disposal, would be subject to regulation.

Technical Assistance for Small Businesses

The previous RCRA draft included a provision directing

the Environmental Protection Agency to develop a technical assistance program to help small businesses meet environmental goals. The language, however, was vague, providing no eligibility guidelines or indication of what elements of compliance should be covered. If the 103rd Congress does alter RCRA, a small business compliance assistance program's purpose should be clearly defined and should include: technical assistance with compliance, access to "no fault" audits, enforcement flexibility, limits on continuous monitoring and representation by small business owners on state compliance advisory panels.

Recycling

The RCRA legislation of the 102nd Congress set up waste-recovery standards for manufacturers of paper, plastic, glass and aluminum. It proposed that manufacturers who do not achieve the established rates should be forced to meet minimum content standards in their packaging. This legislation is not expected to directly affect small businesses, but it could do some indirect harm.

As manufacturers seek to meet their recovery goals, they may institute "take back" programs. These could force businesses carrying their products to collect and store the manufacturers' used packaging. Most small businesses would not have the existing capability or resources to do this. However, since this solution is voluntary in nature, it is preferable to mandated recycling regulations. But both President Clinton and Vice President Gore are on record as strongly favoring a mandated approach.

Community Right to Know More

A possible provision of RCRA harmful to small business is the proposed Community Right to Know More legislation, which seeks to expand the Emergency Planning and Community Right to Know Act of 1986. The original act established annual toxic chemical reporting requirements for 320 substances. It applies to facilities in 19 SIC codes, mainly manufacturers, who employ 10 or more people. Also, coverage is restricted to those facilities that generate 25,000 pounds per year or use 10,000 pounds per year of any one of the listed chemicals.

The new Right to Know More legislation seeks to expand reporting and handling requirements. It would:

- Significantly lower reporting thresholds;
- Expand reportable substances from 320 to 570;
- Expand coverage to 17 additional SIC codes, with more to be included at regular intervals; and
- Require "peak release reports" potentially requiring hourly monitoring of possible chemical releases.

Businesses covered by the legislation include bakeries, gas stations, dry cleaners, auto body repair shops, pharmacies and restaurants. The legislation is expected to increase the number of covered businesses from 29,000 to more than 100,000, which would greatly increase the government expenditure to receive and process the reports.

Even if small businesses don't meet the lowered threshold of chemical releases, they will be required to monitor and evaluate chemical use to determine whether they do meet it. This is a costly process. The EPA estimates reporting now costs businesses $147 million. Industry estimates put that figure closer to $450 million.

If the 103rd Congress does face another RCRA reauthorization measure that includes a Community Right to Know More provision, small business owners should fight against it.

11

What Small Business Owners Must Do

As this book has detailed, the government-imposed barriers which must be overcome by small businesses to survive and succeed seem to grow higher each day.

Small business owners can't take it anymore.

They are fighting back. As individuals, they are getting involved in the political process, making it a point to know personally their elected officials, even running for office themselves.

As a group, they are joining together in record numbers to make their voice heard in their state capitals and in Washington.

The oldest, largest and most effective voice of small business in Washington is NFIB, the National Federation of Independent Business. And with more than 600,000 voices in unison, NFIB delivers a chorus Capitol Hill and the White House listen to.

Founded in 1943, NFIB was created to help protect the free-enterprise system and to give a voice to small and independent business who, unlike large corporations, cannot individually afford spokespersons to explain their concerns to legislators.

But the first step of joining NFIB isn't the only step a small business owner should take. As an NFIB member, there are many actions you can take to help yourself and your colleagues fight for small businesses.

Here are few:

Get to Know Your Legislator

If you are already acquainted with your elected officials, you are well ahead of the game. Having a personal relationship with your state and federal lawmakers is the best way to convey your interests. But lawmakers aren't mind readers. You've still got to tell them what those interests are and provide good reasons to back them up. If you do know your elected official, contact NFIB about its grassroots "Key Contact" program, which helps members make their interests known to state and federal legislators.

If you are not acquainted with your lawmakers, there is no time like the present to introduce yourself. This is especially true if your legislator is newly elected. Seize this opportunity before that person gets too entrenched in Washington or the state capital.

And always remember: no one is elected in Washington. The votes are cast at home, and that's where you should make your individual voice heard. Getting to know your elected officials now, in his or her home district, may help assure better access to them when they are in the middle of a session and voting on legislation important to your business.

Where to start? It's often as easy as calling the official's office, asking when he or she will be in the area, and requesting an appointment. On the phone or in a letter, explain that you are a business owner within the representative's district and that you wish to discuss your positions on certain issues or legislation that you expect to be addressed by the legislative body.

Business owners have especially important perspectives to bring to their legislators. Your business has a direct impact on the economic health of your community, and it is up to you to communicate your insights to lawmakers. The best way to do this is in person. You may wish to include one or two friends who are also small business owners in the meeting. This adds the power of numbers to your position, but should be handled carefully to avoid creating a confrontational atmosphere.

When you call for an appointment, make clear from the outset who you are and why your views are important. Obviously, just being a constituent makes you important, but there is other significant information you should bring forward. Add for example a fact about your business: "I've run an auto parts store in this area for 10 years, and I think the congressman should know how his actions in Washington will affect my business and the 12 people I employ." Or mention your previous support: "I contributed to the congressman's campaign because I knew he would best represent small business owners like me."

Even if all you did was vote for the legislator, say so. And if you voted for his or her opponent, don't worry. Most lawmakers are optimistic that once you get to know them, you can become a future supporter.

It is also good to be specific about the issues that concern you most. If you want to talk about health care reform or environmental regulations or striker replacement legislation, say so. Limit yourself to one or two topics at a time, don't try to hit them all at once.

Plan B Works Too

Sometimes, however, it is not as simple as making a phone request. Scheduling a face-to-face meeting between two busy people can be quite difficult. If you are unable to meet with the legislator, ask to meet with the aide assigned to the specific issue about which you are concerned. Becoming a personal acquaintance with an aide can eventually lead to a direct meeting with your legislator.

Staff members are important to any organization, but they are particularly vital in a congressional and senatorial office. Members of Congress are required to vote on so many issues of such a technical nature that they rely heavily on their staffs to provide information on which they can base their decisions. The staffer you meet may likely be the person who can slice through the bureaucratic red tape when you need to communicate your views on a critical issue to your elected official.

The Public Interest

When you call a legislator's office, you might also ask when the legislator is planning a "town meeting" or other public forum. Federal legislators schedule regular work periods in their home district for the purpose of meeting with their constituents. These are excellent opportunities to introduce yourself and your views to your Washington representatives. Hometown meetings are important because they serve to remind legislators exactly how they gained their offices and to whom they are responsible.

Such meetings are usually well attended, so you may only get the chance to ask one question. However, arriving early and staying late might also afford the chance for a more personal introduction to the legislator or an important aide. If you get that chance, be brief and professional in stating your concerns and in requesting a private meeting. Keep in mind that patient, professional persistence pays off.

Preparing for a Face-to-Face

When you do meet with your legislator or staffer, arrive prepared. Treat this person's time as preciously as your own. Know the issues and present your position clearly, concisely and cordially. Begin with a commendation, if appropriate, and maintain a good-natured, businesslike conversation, even if it becomes apparent that the legislator disagrees with you. People are naturally more receptive to calm, reasoned and constructive criticism than to harsh words.

Develop three key points you'd like to make and use specific examples to illustrate them. For example: "My company and my employees pay more than $50,000 a year in health insurance coverage and we can't afford any more. Your vote on health care reform could force me to lay off valuable people." Remember, if you present your case well, your opinion may be solicited on future key issues, even if you are not successful on the current one.

If you need background information on any issue, state or federal, NFIB can help. On state issues, you can call your state director (check the NFIB state phone directory in the following "Survival Guide" chapter.) For federal issues, NFIB members can call the legislative staff at NFIB's Washington office, (202) 554-9000.

The Volunteer Spirit

If you find your representative to be responsive to your concerns, let him or her know your plans to continue your political support — because you know he or she will continue to keep the interests of small business at the forefront of legislative debate. And don't let your words be mere lip service. Volunteer your time to help.

Ask to become a member of the legislator's business advisory board, so that you can keep the office informed of how hometown voters view pending legislation that affects small businesses and the community at large. Always leave a door open for renewed contact.

The Pen is Mightier

If you are unable to meet with your legislator or an aide, do not give up. The first contact may need to come in writing. While a letter is not as effective as a personal meeting, it could eventually lead to one. And it is a way to get your views on specific matters counted. This is especially important when time is a factor. If the legislator is facing an upcoming vote on legislation important to you, and you cannot schedule a meeting before that time, sending in your "vote yes" or "vote no" is critical.

Again, stick to one subject to keep the length moderate. This will also increase the likelihood of receiving an individualized response instead of a standard form letter. Give reasoned arguments punctuated with "real world" examples from your business experience. Conclude your letter with a clear call to action. Tell your legislator exactly what you want done, for example, a vote for or against a certain bill, or introduction of specific legislation.

If you are not sure how to word your letter, NFIB can offer advice and additional background information. Do not be taken aback if your official answers your letter with a standard form reply. The vast amount of mail legislators receive makes this a necessity for all but a few select letters. Any response puts the ball in your court, so hit it right back. Treat the reply letter as another opportunity to respond to the legislator, either with another letter or, preferably, in person. The key is to pursue an active dialogue.

The Media is an Effective Tool

Besides bringing your views to legislators' attention privately, be sure to raise the issue publicly, as well. The more public comment you spark, the better. While they are serving in Washington or at the state capital, elected officials keep in touch with constituent opinions through their hometown media. Writing a letter to the editor of your local newspaper or TV station is a good way to open a dialogue on any issue. Such letters should be brief but cover the issue well. Use a reasoned, non-combative tone, and provide everyday examples to back up your arguments.

Local applications of national issues are the angle editors seek. Indeed, the difficulty your company is facing may be just the story a reporter or producer needs to have a local spin on a national news story.

Don't be surprised if your letter to the editor or TV station has a ripple effect, drawing responses from the media as well as its readers and viewers. To those that disagree, offer a thoughtful reply in a professional, non-hostile manner. Do your best to keep the issue alive to better catch the attention of legislative readers.

Do not view the media as an enemy. In general, most reporters try to be as accurate as possible. The fact is, they are often reporting on issues they themselves do not completely understand. So, some responsibility for the accuracy of a story must rest with the person originating the story. Therefore, it is very important to learn to communicate effectively with the media. They must ask background questions that may seem obvious to you, but taking the time to cover the issue thoroughly will ultimately benefit your position.

To those who are asked to be interviewed on camera, experts offer a few good guidelines for the uninitiated: Wear solid colors and maintain eye contact with the interviewer. Glancing about to people off camera gives subjects a shifty-eyed appearance. Use controlled, deliberate hand and arm movements to emphasize your point and to show enthusiasm, but do not overdo it or you will appear restless. Be natural. Relax.

When dealing with print or broadcast reporters, always keep the lines of communication open, and be respectful of deadlines. Keep in mind that reporters remember good sources of information. Your helpful attitude on the present story may mean media access on future key issues.

Word of Mouth

Participation in community service groups, religious organizations, special interest clubs and student associations can be very rewarding. It is also an effective way to help publicize the interests of small business. From informal conversation to public speaking, "word of mouth" travels far.

Of course, the idea of standing up before an audience to deliver a formal speech can be frightening to many. Granted, it is not for everybody. But you can learn how to channel that natural nervous energy into contagious enthusiasm. With study and practice, you can learn to approach a lectern with confidence. Most community colleges offer courses in public speaking, and many civic organizations, such as Toastmasters, promote public speaking skills. If the speech is to be covered by the media, hand out typed, double-spaced copies of your speech beforehand, to ensure you are quoted accurately.

Why Not Run Yourself?

If the public speaking or political action bug bites you, don't fight it! NFIB has quite a few members inside state and federal capitals, and the small business community can benefit from more. Many of those members now in legislatures across the country thought the very idea of running for elected office was crazy at the time. But when an incumbent legislator isn't serving the needs of the community, who will? The answer might just be you. If your path leads that way, your first step should be to contact NFIB for advice and assistance.

Don't Just Stand There

No matter how you choose to be involved, the important thing is that you stay involved. Whether you run for office or just maintain your NFIB membership, you are making a difference. Your participation in the system ensures the continuance of small business' big voice in Washington.

The concerns of small business are the concerns of the nation. It is your legislator's duty to represent your views. It is your duty to communicate those views to your legislator.

12

Small Business Survival Guide

It takes idealism, courage, tenacity and an entrepreneurial spirit to own or run a small business. Small business owners dream of watching their hard work flourish and turn into something more profitable and more successful than it was when they began. Small business ownership is about building dreams as much as it is about creating jobs.

In this chapter, you will find the names, the organizations and some of the words you'll need to survive and succeed in the coming years. The outlook for many issues important to small business is bright. President Clinton has pledged to work hard to ensure the job and dream creation machine that is American small business will not be sold out to special interest groups and hidden taxes.

There are still some issues, however, around which small business advocates will need to join together to make their voices heard and their opinions known. It is only through this common effort and a carefully orchestrated strategy that small business interests will be taken seriously.

The previous chapter outlined how small business owners can get involved in lobbying for their cause. This chapter is devoted to the specifics of such efforts. Please use it as a handbook for making your opinions known and for ensuring that future generations have the same chance at individual success that you have had.

The National Federation of Independent Business

More than 99 percent of all businesses in America are small and independent businesses. The participation of every individual business owner is vital to influencing the political machine that affects all small business in America. But when individuals stand together, they carry more political weight, so Big Government will better hear you — and Big Business and Big Labor will think twice before they try to push you around.

The National Federation of Independent Business (NFIB) is a unified, powerful voice for all business owners like you. Because it is the largest, oldest and most effective organization of its kind, it has the collective clout of more than 600,000 members on its side to challenge state and federal legislation detrimental to your business.

NFIB is the nation's largest lobbying staff of its kind, with more than 75 state and federal lobbyists, and offices in every state capital and Washington, D.C. Perhaps most importantly, all stances NFIB takes on legislative issues are determined by member response to surveys. Membership in NFIB allows you to present the views of small and independent business before state and federal legislators with powerful facts, relevant research and the authority and collective clout of the members' votes on the issues. If you are not a member, see the membership enrollment form on the last page of this book to join, or contact one of the offices listed below. You may also telephone 1-800-274-NFIB (6342) for more information.

NFIB State Directors' Offices

Alabama
400 S. Union Street, Suite 465
Montgomery, AL 36104
Tel: 205-264-2261
Fax: 205-264-4252

Alaska
9159 Skywood Lane
Juneau, AK 99801
Tel: 907-789-4278
Fax: 907-789-3433

Arizona
101 W. Almeria
Phoenix, AZ 85003
Tel: 602-254-1541
Fax: 602-254-0354

Arkansas
221 West Second, Suite 621
Little Rock, AR 72201
Tel: 501-372-7593
Fax: 501-375-6001

California
980 9th Street, 16th Floor
Sacramento, CA 95814-2736
Tel: 916-448-9904
Fax: 916-448-5442

Colorado
1410 Grant Street, B104
Denver, CO 80203
Tel: 303-860-1778
Fax: 303-860-1787

Connecticut
88 Palmer Drive
South Windsor, CT 06074
Tel: 203-648-9201
Fax: 203-644-9950 (Call first)

Delaware
P.O. Box 504
Dover, DE 19901
Tel: 302-734-2275
Fax: 302-734-5164

Florida
One Capital Place
110 East Jefferson Street
Tallahassee, FL 32301
Tel: 904-681-0416
Fax: 904-561-6759

Georgia
1447 Peachtree St. N.E.
#1008
Atlanta, GA 30309
Tel: 404-876-8516
Fax: 404-876-1253

Hawaii
1588 Piikea
Honolulu, HI 96818
Tel: 808-422-2163
Fax: 808-422-2163

Idaho
277 N. 6th Street, Suite 200
Boise, ID 83702
Tel: 208-343-3289
Fax: 208-343-1368

Illinois
217 East Monroe Street
Suite 98A
Springfield, IL 62701
Tel: 217-523-5471
Fax: 217-523-3850

Indiana
101 West Ohio Street
Suite 570
Indianapolis, IN 46204
Tel: 317-638-4447
Fax: 317-638-4450

Iowa
319 E. 5th Street
Des Moines, IA 50309
Tel: 515-243-4723
Fax: 515-244-8143

Kansas
10039 Mastin Drive
Shawnee Mission, KS 66212
Tel: 913-888-2235

Kentucky
1501 Twilight Trail
Frankfort, KY 40601
Tel: 502-223-5322
Fax: 502-223-5322 (Call First)

Louisiana
8738 Quarters Lake Road
Suite 5
Baton Rouge, LA 70809
Tel: 504-922-9165
Fax: 504-922-9125

Maine
P.O. Box 4629
Portland, ME 04112-4629
Tel: 207-773-3326
Fax: 207-871-7597

Maryland
7910 Woodmont Ave.
Suite 1204
Bethesda, MD 20814
Tel: 301-652-0721
Fax: 301-657-1973

Small Business Survival Guide

Massachusetts
101 Tremont Street
Suite 1001
Boston, MA 02108
Tel: 617-482-1327
Fax: 617-482-5286

Michigan
114 So. Grand Ave., Suite B
Lansing, MI 48933
Tel: 517-485-3409
Fax: 517-485-2155

Minnesota
26 E. Exchange St., Suite 319
St. Paul, MN 55101
Tel: 612-293-1283
Fax: 612-293-0084

Mississippi
3000 N. State St.
Jackson, MS 39216
Tel: 601-982-3332
Fax: 601-362-2909 (Sir Speedy)

Missouri
P.O. Box 1543
Jefferson City, MO 65102
Tel: 314-634-7660
Fax: 314-636-9749

Montana
491 South Park Ave.
Helena, MT 59601
Tel: 406-443-3797
Fax: 406-442-2107

Nebraska
525 South 13th Street, Suite 3
Lincoln, NE 68508
Tel: 402-474-3570
Fax: 402-474-2946

Nevada
301 W. Washington Street
Suite 2
Carson City, NV 89703
Tel: 702-883-1312
Fax: 702-883-1312

New Hampshire
P.O. Box 218
Concord, NH 03301
Tel: 603-228-3477
Fax: 603-226-0979

New Jersey
156 W. State Street
Trenton, NJ 08608
Tel: 609-989-8777
Fax: 609-393-0781

New Mexico
P.O. Box B546
Santa Fe, NM 87505
Tel: 505-471-5455
Fax: 505-471-5455 (call first)

New York
134 State Street, Suite 400
Albany, NY 12207
Tel: 518-434-1262
Fax: 518-426-8799

North Carolina
P.O. Box 710
Raleigh, NC 27602
Tel: 919-755-1166
Fax: 919-839-1492

North Dakota
1910 N. 11th Street, Suite 10
Bismarck, ND 58501
Tel: 701-224-8333
Fax: 701-223-8746

Ohio
50 West Broad Street
Suite 1321
Columbus, OH 43215
Tel: 614-221-4107
Fax: 614-221-8677

Oklahoma
515 Central Park Drive
Suite 403
Oklahoma City, OK 73105
Tel: 405-521-8967
Fax: 405-528-1462

Oregon
1241 State Street, Suite 211
Salem, OR 97301
Tel: 503-364-4450
Fax: 503-363-5814

Pennsylvania
City Towers, #809
301 Chestnut Street
Harrisburg, PA 17101
Tel: 717-232-8582
Fax: 717-232-4098

Rhode Island
159 Elmgrove Avenue
Providence, RI 02906
Tel: 401-421-8676
Fax: 401-421-3924

South Carolina
P.O. Box 244
Lexington, SC 29072
Tel: 803-359-6300
Fax: 803-359-3265

South Dakota
319 Coteau Street, Box 280
Pierre, SD 57501
Tel: 605-224-7102
Fax: 605-224-7102 (Call first)

Tennessee
53 Century Blvd., Suite 300
Nashville, TN 37214
Tel: 615-872-5855
Fax: 615-872-5899

Texas
815 Brazos Bldg., Suite 900
Austin, TX 78701
Tel: 512-476-9847
Fax: 512-478-6422

Utah
1756 East 10980 South
Sandy, UT 84092
Tel: 801-571-1171
Fax: 801-571-1271

Vermont
RR #1, Box 3517
Montpelier, VT 05602
Tel: 802-229-9478
Fax: 802-229-2745

Virginia
700 E. Main Street
Suite #1623
Richmond, VA 23219
Tel: 804-643-0043
Fax: 804-788-0447

Washington
509 East 12th Ave., Suite 8
Olympia, WA 98501
Tel: 206-786-8675
Fax: 206-943-2456

West Virginia
2253 Miller Road
Huntington, WV 25701
Tel: 304-529-3471
Fax: 304-529-3471 (Call first)

Wisconsin
119 M.L. King, Jr. Blvd.
Suite 516
Madison, WI 53703
Tel: 608-255-6083
Fax: 608-255-4909

Wyoming
1805 Capitol Ave., Suite 201
Cheyenne, WY 82001
Tel: 307-778-4045
Fax: 307-638-3469

NFIB Board of Directors

James S. Herr
Herr Foods, Inc.
Box 300
Nottingham, PA 19362

Susan A. Andrews
Brookside Properties, Inc.
224 White Bridge Road
Nashville, TN 37209

Ramon E. Billeaud
J.B. Levert Land Co.
P.O. Box 19245
New Orleans, LA 70179

Richard S. Briggs
307 Olive Hill Lane
Woodside, CA 94062

S. Jackson Faris
NFIB
53 Century Blvd., Suite 300
Nashville, TN 37214

Bruce G. Fielding, C.P.A.
Fielding & Associates
246A Center Avenue
Aptos, CA 95003

Mary F. Kelley
Strait, Kushinsky and Company
1050 17th Street, Suite 1900
Denver, CO 80265-1901

Richard L. Reinhardt
PII Affiliates, Ltd.
P.O. Box 577
Manchester, PA 17345

Sidney T. Small
Sidmar Enterprises, Inc.
Two Kleen Way
Holbrook, MA 02343

William G. Thornton Jr.
Thornton Gardens
510 East U.S. 22 & 3
Maineville, OH 45039

Effective Letter Writing

O.K., so you've decided to get involved. To take personal measures to influence pro-small business public policy. But how do you make sure out of the thousands of letters a public official receives, your letter makes an impression? The following guidelines should help you:

- Timeliness Counts.

Very often, you can help a legislator form opinions on new legislation if you write a thoughtful, well-reasoned letter during the early stages of deliberation on a bill. It is more likely, however, that you will hear about pending legislation just before it is up for a vote. It is at this time that a quick response on your part will actually affect the outcome of the legislative roll call.

- Identify Yourself.

Use your business or personal letterhead whenever possible, providing your full name, business name, address and telephone number. Type your full name just below your signature. Use your judgment about which aspects of your background will most interest your legislator. For example, you might say, " I have owned my business for 25 years and have employed more than 150 local people during that time, so I understand the issues facing small business."

If you are a member of a trade association or other organization, such as the NFIB, that supports your views, mention it. For example, you might say, "I'm a member of the Printers Association of America and its position on workmen's compensation is the same as mine."

• Style Matters.

When lobbying for your cause, take the time to address the public official by his or her proper title. The following is the correct way to address such officials:

President of the United States
The President
The White House
Washington, D.C.
Dear Mr. President:

Cabinet Secretary
The Honorable Jane Doe
Secretary of Commerce
U.S. Department of Commerce
Washington, D.C.
Dear Mr. Secretary:
Dear Madam Secretary:

U.S. Senator
The Honorable John Doe
United States Senate
Washington, D.C.
Dear Senator Doe:

U.S. Representative
The Honorable Jane Doe
U.S. House of Representatives
Washington, D.C.
Dear Congresswoman Doe:
Dear Congressman Doe:

Governor
The Honorable John Doe
Governor of Colorado
State House (or State Capitol)
Denver, Colorado
Dear Governor Doe:

State Legislator
The Honorable Jane Doe
Ohio House of Representatives
or Ohio State Senate
State House (or State Capitol)
Columbus, Ohio
Dear Senator Doe:
Dear Representative Doe:

Mayor
The Honorable John Doe
Mayor of Atlanta
City Hall
Atlanta, Georgia
Dear Mayor Doe:

Be sure to personalize your letter. You can even write it by hand, if it is legible; handwritten letters are often more effective than typed ones. State your case clearly and succinctly.

Don't try to address more than one issue per letter, and stick to the major points you wish to make about that issue.

Try to connect your topic with news items or some other timely issue. For example, you might say, "The national unemployment figures released yesterday indicate that we must do something to support small businesses, since they create two out of every three new jobs in this country."

- Know the Issue

Write in your own words. An original letter always carries more weight than a form letter. If you are using arguments from NFIB or another lobbying organization's material, do not copy them verbatim. Change the wording, list the reasons in a different order, or choose one or two reasons and explain how they relate to your business and community.

It's also important to mention bill numbers if you are discussing legislation. (NFIB can help with details like these.) Quite often, several bills all relating to the same problem will be under consideration at the same time, and each bill will represent a slightly different approach to solving the problem.

- **Know Who to Contact**

  It's best to write your own representative rather than someone from another area. Exceptions might occur when you write to someone who is running for the presidency or to someone who is on a committee studying the legislation or issue which concerns you.

- **Positive Words.**

  Begin your letter with a commendation if at all appropriate, and maintain a calm, reasoned tone in your letter. People are naturally more receptive to constructive criticism than to harsh words. Therefore, a brief explanation of how you reached your conclusion and what alternatives are available are good points to include.

- **Be Specific.**

  Tell your legislator exactly what action you would like taken on the issue, whether it involves voting a certain way or introducing specific legislation. A summary or conclusion will ensure that your remarks are clearly understood and not subject to misinterpretation.

- **Following Through is Key**

  A follow-up letter is crucial whenever you've had contact with your legislator. Legislators often have standard letters they send in response to contacts from their constituents. When you follow up their standard letters and highlight points they've made in them, you force them to think further and respond to you again.

For example, you may receive a letter from your legislator that states, "I agree with you that escalating health insurance premiums are a problem. But until we can control the inflation of medical costs, we will not see a decrease in premiums."

You could respond to that letter as follows: "Thank you, Congressman Doe, for your letter. I appreciated your thoughts about escalating health care costs; however, did you know that..."

When your legislator casts a vote that supports your position, always follow up with a letter of appreciation. A follow-up letter in this case will let the elected official know that you're aware of how he or she voted on the issues.

Be sure to keep copies of your letters and responses, and please forward copies of them to lobbying organizations you support, such as **NFIB**.

Small Business Survival Guide

The NFIB Foundation-Southwestern Bell Small Business Help-Line*

For up-to-date information on issues concerning small businesses, call the Small Business Help-Line, sponsored by the NFIB Foundation and Southwestern Bell. It's easy to use and updated frequently. Need helpful ideas for your business? Interested in the latest small business-related news from Washington? Now, it's only a phone call away.

1-900-820-6342
(Touch Tone phones ONLY)

The cost is 95 cents per minute. All revenues are used to develop, expand and promote the Small Business Help-Line.

When calling, use this "message menu" as your guide for more information on the Small Business Help-Line. Simply press the two-digit code on your phone when directed by the operator:

Forming a Business
01. Getting started in business.
02. Writing a business plan.
09. Sources of free and inexpensive information for your new business.

Finance
11. Getting a bank loan for your small business.
12. Choosing a bank for your small business.
14. The money connection: sources of small business financing.
16. Managing cash flow.
18. Billing and collection for your small business.

Personnel
20. Employer obligations.
22. Payroll tax obligations for small business employers.
24. Reducing your health insurance costs.
25. Hiring independent contractors.
28. Motivating your employees.

Marketing
30. Identifying your market.
33. Cost-effective advertising ideas for your small business.
36. 7 steps to outstanding customer service.
39. Telephone etiquette: making a good impression.

Management
41. Increasing your competitiveness.
42. Cost-cutting ideas for your small business.

Current Topics
50. What's going on in Washington.
51. When the IRS calls.
54. The Americans with Disabilities Act and your small business.
59. Small business' advocate: the National Federation of Independent Business

*Sponsored by The NFIB Foundation, Washington, D.C., and Southwestern Bell Telephone, St. Louis, MO. Help-Line message content is the sole responsibility of The NFIB Foundation.

For more information about NFIB and its activities, call toll-free 1-800-274-NFIB. You can also write to: NFIB Membership, 53 Century Boulevard, Suite 205, Nashville, Tennessee 37214.

Opinions of Small Business Owners On Key Issues Facing the Clinton Administration & the 103rd Congress

One of the things that makes NFIB unique among Washington advocacy organizations is that its stance on issues is not determined by a small group of board members and Beltway insiders, but by the votes of its entire membership. Several times each year, NFIB sends its more than 600,000 members a survey asking their position on key public policy issues which have direct impact on their businesses. The response to these "Mandate" surveys is overwhelming, with more than 100,000 business owners responding to each mailing.

These surveys are more than merely opinion research, they are the ballots with which the entire membership mandates the stance NFIB takes in Washington when lobbying on behalf of small business owners.

The diverse opinions received in response to these surveys will dispel the claims of adversaries who characterize small business owners as a narrow "special interest group."

The following are NFIB member votes/positions on some of the key issues discussed in this book, and expected to be considered by the Clinton administration and the 103rd Congress.

The Budget, the Deficit & Taxes

Should the top income-tax rates be increased to help meet next year's budget deficit target ?
(Mandate 483)

>Favor: 16%
>Oppose: 81%
>Undecided: 3%

Should a freeze be imposed on the federal budget?
(Mandate 479)

>Favor: 72%
>Oppose: 18%
>Undecided: 10%

Should reductions in the Department of Defense budget be used to cut taxes? (Mandate 485)

>Favor: 66%
>Oppose: 39%
>Undecided: 5%

Small Business Owner Opinions

Should Congress focus its attention primarily on: deficit reduction, foreign affairs, domestic programs, or none of the above? (Mandate 491)

Deficit reduction: 88%
Domestic programs: 10%
Foreign affairs: 1%
None of the above: 1%

How should Congress reduce the deficit? (Mandate 471)

Tax stock transactions and cut spending: 19%
Cut spending: 71%
Increase the gasoline tax and cut spending: 8%
None of the above: 2%

Should the federal gasoline tax be increased 15 to 20 cents per gallon to reduce the deficit? (Mandate 479)

Favor: 23%
Oppose: 71%
Undecided: 6%

Should the investment tax credit be reinstated for small firms? (Mandate 495)

Favor: 81%
Oppose: 11%
Undecided: 8%

Child Labor

Should child labor laws be strengthened? (Mandate 489)

> Favor: 20%
> Oppose: 68%
> Undecided: 12%

Should individuals below the age of 18 be required to obtain work permits? (Mandate 494)

> Favor: 22%
> Oppose: 70%
> Undecided: 8%

Should workers under age 18 be restricted to limited part-time employment to encourage them to stay in school? (Mandate 485)

> Favor: 43%
> Oppose: 51%
> Undecided: 6%

Employee Benefits

Should part-time employees get the same benefits as full-time employees? (Mandate 497)

> Favor: 7%
> Oppose: 90%
> Undecided: 3%

Small Business Owner Opinions

Should employers be required to provide unpaid parental and disability leave? (Mandate 479)

Favor: 9%
Oppose: 84%
Undecided: 7%

Should a tax deduction be given to employers who offer parental leave as an employee benefit? (Mandate 479)

Favor: 35%
Oppose: 57%
Undecided: 8%

Should Congress establish a minimum uniform maternity leave standard? (Mandate 481)

Favor: 9%
Oppose: 83%
Undecided: 8%

Environment

Should polluters, including small businesses, be required to pay a fee to EPA that would be used to enforce the Clean Air Act? (Mandate 484)

Favor: 47%
Oppose: 41%
Undecided: 12%

Should small businesses cited for minor violations of the Clean Air Act have fines suspended for first offenses? (Mandate 486)

    Favor: 78%
    Oppose: 17%
    Undecided: 5%

Should the Endangered Species Act be amended to include equal evaluation of economic and environmental impact? (Mandate 493)

    Favor: 55%
    Oppose: 31%
    Undecided: 14%

Should Congress enact a tax on materials that pollute the environment? (Mandate 497)

    Favor: 30%
    Oppose: 60%
    Undecided: 10%

Should businesses be required to label common products to indicate health and safety hazards? (Mandate 481)

    Favor: 39%
    Oppose: 50%
    Undecided: 11%

Small Business Owner Opinions

Should businesses be required to meet reduction goals for solid and hazardous waste? (Mandate 481)

Favor: 48%
Oppose: 36%
Undecided: 16%

Should Congress require businesses to recycle a certain percentage of their solid waste? (Mandate 492)

Favor: 34%
Oppose: 57%
Undecided: 9%

Health Care

Should employers be required to provide health insurance for their employees? (Mandate 470)

Favor: 8%
Oppose: 88%
Undecided: 4%

Should employers be required to provide health insurance for their employees? (Mandate 481)

Favor: 8%
Oppose: 88%
Undecided: 4%

Should employers with health insurance plans be required to cover former employees who have pre-existing conditions? (Mandate 479)

    Favor: 10%
    Oppose: 83%
    Undecided: 7%

Should employers be required to offer health insurance without having to pay the premiums? (Mandate 494)

    Favor: 30%
    Oppose: 60%
    Undecided: 10%

Should payroll taxes be increased to provide health coverage for the uninsured? (Mandate 483)

    Favor: 4%
    Oppose: 94%
    Undecided: 2%

Should the federal government regulate the health insurance industry? (Mandate 491)

    Favor: 23%
    Oppose: 63%
    Undecided: 14

Small Business Owner Opinions

Should an individual income tax deduction for health insurance be restored? (Mandate 484)

Favor: 75%
Oppose: 17%
Undecided: 8%

If Congress mandates health insurance, should participants be taxed on the value of the premium? (Mandate 478)

Favor: 15%
Oppose: 81%
Undecided: 4%

Should the top corporate tax rate be increased to offset the cost of tax incentives for small business owners to offer health insurance? (Mandate 490)

Favor: 20%
Oppose: 70%
Undecided: 10%

Labor

Should the Davis-Bacon Act be extended to cover all subcontractors and suppliers? (Mandate 496)

Favor: 8%
Oppose: 78%
Undecided: 14%

Should Congress require employers to establish safety committees? Mandate 496)

> Favor: 6%
> Oppose: 86%
> Undecided: 8%

Should Congress enact a federal right-to-work law? (Mandate 497)

> Favor: 62%
> Oppose: 31%
> Undecided: 7%

Occupational Health & Safety

Should OSHA penalties be increased and minimum penalties be established to encourage compliance with safety and health regulations? (Mandate 486)

> Favor: 19%
> Oppose: 72%
> Undecided: 9%

Small Business Owner Opinions

Government Regulation & Paperwork Reduction

Should the Paperwork Reduction Act apply to paperwork that the government requires business owners to retain? (Mandate 490)

> Favor: 67%
> Oppose: 13%
> Undecided: 20%

Should federal agencies be required to assess whether a regulation could restrict the use of private property? (Mandate 490)

> Favor: 64%
> Oppose: 18%
> Undecided: 18%

Should EPA be required to produce a "small business impact statement" when writing new environmental regulations? (Mandate 487)

> Favor: 76%
> Oppose: 13%
> Undecided: 11%

Term Limits

Should the Constitution be amended to limit the terms of U.S. Senators and Representatives? (Mandate 482)

> Favor: 66%
> Oppose: 26%
> Undecided: 8%

Congressional Directory

The following list of members of the 103rd Congress will help you decide to whom to send your correspondence.

The most effective way to contact your senator or representative is through his or her home office, where they are elected. We have listed the U.S. Capitol phone numbers of the 103rd Congress for a central reference. Central Washington addresses for senators and representatives are as follows:

U.S. Senate
Washington, D.C. 20510

U.S. House of Representatives
Washington, D.C. 20515

Alabama
Senate:
Howell Heflin (D)	202-224-4124
Richard C. Shelby (D)	202-224-5744

House:
1	Sonny Callahan (R)	202-225-4931
2	*Terry Everett (R)	
3	Glen Browder (D)	202-225-3261
4	Tom Bevill (D)	202-225-4876
5	Bud Cramer (D)	202-225-4801

It is always better to contact your congressional representative in his or her home office. You will find that number in your local directory. *New members. Contact U.S. Capitol: 202-224-3121.

6   *Spencer Bachus (R)
7   *Earl Hilliard (D)

Alaska
Senate:
Frank H. Murkowski (R)   202-224-6665
Ted Stevens (R)   202-224-3004

House:
At Large, Don Young (R)   202-225-5765

Arizona
Senate:
Dennis DeConcini (D)   202-224-4521
John McCain (R)   202-224-2235

House:
1   *Sam Coppersmith (D)
2   Ed Pastor (D)   202-225-4065
3   Bob Stump (R)   202-225-4576
4   Jon Kyl (R)   202-225-3361
5   Jim Kolbe (R)   202-225-2542
6   *Karan English (D)

Arkansas
Senate:
Dale L. Bumpers (D)   202-224-4843
David H. Pryor (D)   202-224-2353

House:
1   *Blanche Lambert (D)
2   Ray Thornton (D)   202-225-2506
3   *Tim Hutchinson (R)
4   *Jay Dickey (R)

California
Senate:
*Barbara Boxer (D)
*Dianne Feinstein (D)

House:
1   *Dan Hamburg (D)
2   Wally Herger (R)   202-225-3076
3   Vic Fazio (D)   202-225-5716
4   John Doolittle (R)   202-225-2511
5   Robert T. Matsui (D)   202-225-7163

It is always better to contact your congressional representative in his or her home office. You will find that number in your local directory. *New members. Contact U.S. Capitol: 202-224-3121.

Congressional Directory

6	*Lynn Woolsey (D)	
7	George Miller (D)	202-225-2095
8	Nancy Pelosi (D)	202-225-4965
9	Ronald V. Dellums (D)	202-225-2661
10	*Bill Baker (R)	
11	*Richard Pombo (R)	
12	Tom Lantos (D)	202-225-3531
13	Fortney Stark (D)	202-225-5065
14	*Anna Eshoo (D)	
15	Norman Mineta (D)	202-225-2631
16	Don Edwards (D)	202-225-3072
17	Leon Panetta (D)	202-225-2861
18	Gary Condit (D)	202-225-6131
19	Rick Lehman (D)	202-225-4540
20	Calvin Dooley (D)	202-225-3341
21	Bill Thomas (R)	202-225-2915
22	*Michael Huffington (R)	
23	Elton Gallegly (R)	202-225-5811
24	Anthony C. Beilenson (D)	202-225-5911
25	*Howard McKeon (R)	
26	Howard L. Berman (D)	202-225-4695
27	Carlos J. Moorhead (R)	202-225-4176
28	David Dreier (R)	202-225-2305
29	Henry A. Waxman (D)	202-225-3976
30	*Xavier Becerra (D)	
31	Matthew G. Martinez (D)	202-225-5464
32	Julian C. Dixon (D)	202-225-7084
33	*Lucille Roybal-Allard (D)	
34	Esteban Torres (D)	202-225-5256
35	Maxine Waters (D)	202-225-2201
36	*Jane Harman (D)	
37	*Walter Tucker (D)	
38	*Steve Horn (R)	
39	*Edward Royce (R)	
40	Jerry Lewis (R)	202-225-5861
41	*Jay Kim (R)	
42	George Brown Jr. (D)	202-225-6161
43	*Ken Calvert (R)	
44	Al McCandless (R)	202-225-5330
45	Dana Rohrabacher (R)	202-225-2415
46	Robert Dornan (R)	202-225-2965
47	Christopher Cox (R)	202-225-5611
48	Ron Packard (R)	202-225-3906
49	*Lynn Schenk (D)	
50	*Bob Filner (D)	
51	Randy Cunningham (R)	202-225-5452

It is always better to contact your congressional representative in his or her home office. You will find that number in your local directory. *New members. Contact U.S. Capitol: 202-224-3121.

52 Duncan Hunter (R)   202-225-5672

Colorado
Senate:
Hank Brown (R)   202-224-5941
*Ben Nighthorse Campbell (D)

House:
1 Pat Schroeder (D)   202-225-4431
2 David E. Skaggs (D)   202-225-2161
3 *Scott McInnis (R)
4 Wayne Allard (R)   202-225-4676
5 Joel M. Hefley (R)   202-225-4422
6 Dan Schaefer (R)   202-225-7882

Connecticut
Senate:
Christopher J. Dodd (D)   202-224-2823
Joseph I. Lieberman (D)   202-224-4041

House:
1 Barbara B. Kennelly (D)   202-225-2265
2 Sam Gejdenson (D)   202-225-2076
3 Rosa DeLauro (D)   202-225-3661
4 Christopher Shays (R)   202-225-5541
5 Gary Franks (R)   202-225-3822
6 Nancy Johnson (R)   202-225-4476

Delaware
Senate:
Joseph R. Biden Jr. (D)   202-224-5042
William V. Roth Jr. (R)   202-224-2441

House:
At Large, *Michael Castle (R)

Florida
Senate:
Bob Graham (D)   202-224-3041
Connie Mack (R)   202-224-5274

House:
1 Earl Hutto (D)   202-225-4136
2 Pete Peterson (D)   202-225-5235
3 *Corrine Brown (D)
4 *Tillie Fowler (R)

It is always better to contact your congressional representative in his or her home office. You will find that number in your local directory. *New members. Contact U.S. Capitol: 202-224-3121.

Congressional Directory

5	*Karen Thurman (D)	
6	Clifford B. Stearns (R)	202-225-5744
7	*John Mica (R)	
8	Bill McCollum (R)	202-225-2176
9	Michael Bilirakis (R)	202-225-5755
10	Bill Young (R)	202-225-5961
11	Sam M. Gibbons (D)	202-225-3376
12	*Charles Canady (R)	
13	*Dan Miller (R)	
14	Porter J. Goss (R)	202-225-2536
15	Jim Bacchus (D)	202-225-3671
16	Tom Lewis (R)	202-225-5729
17	*Carrie Meek (D)	
18	Ileana Ros-Lehtinen (R)	202-225-3931
19	Harry A. Johnston II (D)	202-225-3001
20	*Peter Deutsch (D)	
21	*Lincoln Diaz-Balart (R)	
22	E. Clay Shaw Jr. (R)	202-225-3026
23	*Alcee Hastings (D)	

Georgia
Senate:
*Paul Coverdell (R)
Sam Nunn (D)   202-224-3521

House:
1	*Jack Kingston (R)	
2	*Sanford Bishop (D)	
3	*Mac Collins (R)	
4	*John Linder (R)	
5	John Lewis (D)	202-225-3801
6	Newt Gingrich (R)	202-225-4501
7	Buddy Darden (D)	202-225-2931
8	J. Roy Rowland (D)	202-225-6531
9	*Nathan Deal (D)	
10	*Don Johnson (D)	
11	*Cynthia McKinney (D)	

Hawaii
Senate:
Daniel K. Akaka (D)   202-224-6361
Daniel K. Inouye (D)   202-224-3934

House:
1	Neil Abercrombie (D)	202-225-2726
2	Patsy Mink (D)	202-225-4906

It is always better to contact your congressional representative in his or her home office. You will find that number in your local directory. *New members. Contact U.S. Capitol: 202-224-3121.

Idaho
Senate:
Larry E. Craig (R) 202-224-2752
*Dirk Kempthorne (R)

House:
1   Larry LaRocco (D) 202-225-6611
2   *Michael Crappo (R)

Illinois
Senate:
*Carol Moseley Braun (D)
Paul Simon (D) 202-224-2152

House:
1   *Bobby Rush (D)
2   *Mel Reynolds (D)
3   William Lipinski (D) 202-225-5701
4   *Luis Gutierrez (D)
5   Dan Rostenkowski (D) 202-225-4061
6   Henry J. Hyde (R) 202-225-4561
7   Cardiss Collins (D) 202-225-5006
8   Phillip M. Crane (R) 202-225-3711
9   Sidney R. Yates (D) 202-225-2111
10 John E. Porter (R) 202-225-4835
11 George Sangmeister (D) 202-225-3635
12 Jerry Costello (D) 202-225-5661
13 Harris Fawell (R) 202-225-3515
14 Dennis Hastert (R) 202-225-2976
15 Thomas Ewing (R) 202-225-2371
16 *Donald Manzullo (R)
17 Lane Evans (D) 202-225-5905
18 Robert H. Michel (R) 202-225-6201
19 Glenn Poshard (D) 202-225-5201
20 Richard J. Durbin (D) 202-225-5271

Indiana
Senate:
Dan Coats (R) 202-224-5623
Richard G. Lugar 202-224-4814

House:
1   Peter J. Visclosky (D) 202-225-2461
2   Phillip Sharp (D) 202-225-3021
3   Tim Roemer (D) 202-225-3915
4   Jill Long (D) 202-225-4436

It is always better to contact your congressional representative in his or her home office. You will find that number in your local directory. *New members. Contact U.S. Capitol: 202-224-3121.

5	*Steve Buyer (R)	
6	Dan Burton (R)	202-225-2276
7	John T. Myers (R)	202-225-5805
8	Frank McCloskey (D)	202-225-4636
9	Lee H. Hamilton (D)	202-225-5315
10	Andrew Jacobs Jr. (D)	202-225-4011

Iowa
Senate:
Charles E. Grassley (R)   202-224-3744
Tom Harkin (D)   202-224-3254

House:
1	Jim Leach (R)	202-225-6576
2	Jim Nussle (R)	202-225-2911
3	Jim Lightfoot (R)	202-225-3806
4	Neal Smith (D)	202-225-4426
5	Fred Grandy (R)	202-225-5476

Kansas
Senate:
Bob Dole (R)   202-224-6521
Nancy Landon Kassebaum (R)   202-224-4774

House:
1	Pat Roberts (R)	202-225-2715
2	Jim Slattery (D)	202-225-6601
3	Jan Meyers (R)	202-225-2865
4	Dan Glickman (D)	202-225-6216

Kentucky
Senate:
Wendell H. Ford (D)   202-224-4343
Mitch McConnell (R)   202-224-2541

House:
1	*Tom Barlow (D)	
2	William H. Natcher (D)	202-225-3501
3	Romano L. Mazzoli (D)	202-225-5401
4	Jim Bunning (R)	202-225-3465
5	Harold Rogers (R)	202-225-4601
6	*Scotty Baesler (D)	

It is always better to contact your congressional representative in his or her home office. You will find that number in your local directory. *New members. Contact U.S. Capitol: 202-224-3121.

Louisiana
Senate:
John Breaux (D)	202-224-4623
J. Bennett Johnston (D)	202-224-5824

House:
1	Robert L. Livingston Jr. (R)	202-225-3015
2	William Jefferson (D)	202-225-6636
3	Billy Tauzin (D)	202-225-4031
4	*Cleo Fields (D)	
5	Jim McCrery (R)	202-225-2777
6	Richard Baker (R)	202-225-3901
7	James A. Hayes (D)	202-225-2031

Maine
Senate:
William S. Cohen (R)	202-224-2523
George J. Mitchell (D)	202-224-5344

House
1	Thomas Andrews (D)	202-225-6116
2	Olympia J. Snowe (R)	202-225-6306

Maryland
Senate:
Barbara Mikulski (D)	202-224-4654
Paul Sarbanes (D)	202-224-4524

House:
1	Wayne Gilchrest (R)	202-225-5311
2	Helen Delich Bentley (R)	202-225-3061
3	Benjamin L. Cardin (D)	202-225-4016
4	*Albert Wynn (D)	
5	Steny H. Hoyer (D)	202-225-4131
6	*Roscoe Bartlett (R)	
7	Kweisi Mfume (D)	202-225-4741
8	Connie Morella (R)	202-225-5341

Massachusetts
Senate:
Edward M. Kennedy (D)	202-224-4543
John F. Kerry (D)	202-224-2742

House:
1	John Olver (D)	202-225-5335
2	Richard E. Neal (D)	202-225-5601

It is always better to contact your congressional representative in his or her home office. You will find that number in your local directory. *New members. Contact U.S. Capitol: 202-224-3121.

Congressional Directory

3	*Peter Blute (R)	
4	Barney Frank (D)	202-225-5931
5	*Martin Meehan (D)	
6	*Peter Torkildsen (R)	
7	Edward J. Markey (D)	202-225-2836
8	Joseph P. Kennedy II (D)	202-225-5111
9	Joe Moakley (D)	202-225-8273
10	Gerry E. Studds (D)	202-225-3111

Michigan
Senate:
Carl Levin (D) 202-224-6211
Donald W. Riegle Jr. (D) 202-224-4822

House:
1	*Bart Stupak (D)	
2	*Peter Hoekstra (R)	
3	Paul Henry (R)	202-225-3831
4	Dave Camp (R)	202-225-3561
5	*James Barcia (D)	
6	Fred Upton (R)	202-225-3761
7	*Nick Smith (R)	
8	Bob Carr (D)	202-225-4872
9	Dale Kildee (D)	202-225-3611
10	David Bonior (D)	202-225-2106
11	*Joseph Knollenberg (R)	
12	Sander Levin (D)	202-225-4961
13	William Ford (D)	202-225-6261
14	John Conyers Jr. (D)	202-225-5126
15	Barbara-Rose Collins (D)	202-225-2261
16	John Dingell (D)	202-225-4071

Minnesota
Senate:
Dave Durenberger (R) 202-224-3244
Paul D. Wellstone (D) 202-224-5641

House:
1	Tim Penny (D)	202-225-2472
2	*David Minge (D)	
3	Jim Ramstad (R)	202-225-2871
4	Bruce Vento (D)	202-225-6631
5	Martin Sabo (D)	202-225-4755
6	*Rod Grams (R)	
7	Collin Peterson (D)	202-225-2165
8	James Oberstar (D)	202-225-6211

It is always better to contact your congressional representative in his or her home office. You will find that number in your local directory. *New members. Contact U.S. Capitol: 202-224-3121.

Mississippi
Senate:
Thad Cochran (R)	202-224-5054
Trent Lott (R)	202-224-6253

House
1	James Whitten (D)	202-225-4306
2	Mike Espy (D)	202-225-5876
3	Sonny Montgomery (D)	202-225-5031
4	Mike Parker (D)	202-225-5865
5	Gene Taylor (D)	202-225-5772

Missouri
Senate:
Christopher S. Bond (R)	202-224-5721
John C. Danforth (R)	202-224-6154

House:
1	William Clay Sr. (D)	202-225-2406
2	*James Talent (R)	
3	Richard Gephardt (D)	202-225-2671
4	Ike Skelton (D)	202-225-2876
5	Alan Wheat (D)	202-225-4535
6	*Pat Danner (D)	
7	Mel Hancock (R)	202-225-6536
8	Bill Emerson (R)	202-225-4404
9	Harold Volkmer (D)	202-225-2956

Montana
Senate:
Max Baucus (D)	202-224-2651
Conrad Burns (R)	202-224-2644

House:
At Large, Pat Williams (D)	202-225-3211

Nebraska
Senate:
James J. Exon (D)	202-224-4224
Robert J. Kerrey (D)	202-224-6551

House
1	Doug Bereuter (R)	202-225-4806
2	Peter Hoagland (D)	202-225-4155
3	Bill Barrett (R)	202-225-6435

It is always better to contact your congressional representative in his or her home office. You will find that number in your local directory. *New members. Contact U.S. Capitol: 202-224-3121.

Congressional Directory

Nevada
Senate:
Richard H. Bryan (D)   202-224-6244
Harry M. Reid (D)   202-224-3542

House
1   James H. Bilbray (D)   202-225-5965
2   Barbara F. Vucanovich (R)   202-225-6155

New Hampshire
Senate:
*Judd Gregg (R)
Bob Smith (R)   202-224-2841

House:
1   Bill Zeliff (R)   202-225-5456
2   Dick Swett (D)   202-225-5206

New Jersey
Senate:
Bill Bradley (D)   202-224-3224
Frank R. Lautenberg (D)   202-224-4744

House:
1   Robert Andrews (D)   202-225-6501
2   William J. Hughes (D)   202-225-6572
3   Jim Saxton (R)   202-225-4765
4   Christopher H. Smith (R)   202-225-3765
5   Marge Roukema (R)   202-225-4465
6   Frank Pallone Jr. (D)   202-225-4671
7   *Bob Franks (R)
8   *Herbert Klein (D)
9   Robert G. Torricelli (D)   202-225-5061
10   Donald M. Payne (D)   202-225-3436
11   Dean A. Gallo (R)   202-225-5034
12   Richard A. Zimmer (R)   202-225-5801
13   *Robert Menendez (D)

New Mexico
Senate:
Jeff Bingaman (D)   202-224-5521
Pete V. Domenici (R)   202-224-6621

House
1   Steven Schiff (R)   202-225-6316
2   Joe Skeen (R)   202-225-2365

It is always better to contact your congressional representative in his or her home office. You will find that number in your local directory. *New members. Contact U.S. Capitol: 202-224-3121.

3   Bill Richardson (D)   202-225-6190

New York
Senate:
Alfonse D'Amato (R)   202-224-6542
Daniel Patrick Moynihan (D)   202-224-4451

House:
1   George J. Hochbrueckner (D)   202-225-3826
2   *Rick Lazio (R)
3   *Peter T. King (R)
4   *David Levy (R)
5   Gary L. Ackerman (D)   202-225-2601
6   Floyd H. Flake (D)   202-225-3461
7   Thomas J. Manton (D)   202-225-3965
8   Jerrold Nadler (D)   202-225-5471
9   Charles E. Schumer (D)   202-225-6615
10 Edolphus Towns (D)   202-225-5936
11 Major R. Owens (D)   202-225-6231
12 *Nydia Velazquez (D)
13 Susan Molinari (R)   202-225-3371
14 *Carolyn Maloney (D)
15 Charles B. Rangel (D)   202-225-4365
16 Jose Serrano (D)   202-225-4361
17 Eliot L. Engel (D)   202-225-2464
18 Nita M. Lowey (D)   202-225-6506
19 Hamilton Fish Jr. (R)   202-225-5441
20 Benjamin A. Gilman (R)   202-225-3776
21 Michael R. McNulty (D)   202-225-5076
22 Gerald Solomon (R)   202-225-5614
23 Sherwood L. Boehlert (R)   202-225-3665
24 *John McHugh (R)
25 James T. Walsh (R)   202-225-3701
26 *Maurice Hinchey (D)
27 Bill Paxon (R)   202-225-5265
28 Louise M. Slaughter (D)   202-225-3615
29 John J. LaFalce (D)   202-225-3231
30 *Jack Quinn (R)
31 Amo Houghton Jr. (R)   202-225-3161

North Carolina
Senate:
*Lauch Faircloth (R)
Jesse Helms (R)   202-224-6342

It is always better to contact your congressional representative in his or her home office. You will find that number in your local directory. *New members. Contact U.S. Capitol: 202-224-3121.

Congressional Directory

House:
1 *Eva Clayton (D)
2 Tim Valentine (D)   202-225-4531
3 Martin Lancaster (D)   202-225-3415
4 David E. Price (D)   202-225-1784
5 Steve Neal (D)   202-225-2071
6 Howard Coble (R)   202-225-3065
7 Charles Rose III (D)   202-225-2731
8 Bill Hefner (D)   202-225-3715
9 Alex McMillan (R)   202-225-1976
10 Cass Ballenger (R)   202-225-2576
11 Charles Taylor (R)   202-225-6401
12 *Melvin Watt (D)

North Dakota
Senate:
*Byron Dorgan (D)
*Kent Conrad (D)

House:
At Large, Earl Pomeroy (D)

Ohio
Senate:
John Glenn (D)   202-224-3353
Howard M. Metzenbaum (D)   202-224-2315

House:
1 *David Mann (D)
2 Willis D. Gradison (R)   202-225-3164
3 Tony Hall (D)   202-225-6465
4 Michael G. Oxley (R)   202-225-2676
5 Paul Gillmor (R)   202-225-6405
6 *Ted Strickland (D)
7 David Hobson (R)   202-225-4324
8 John Boehner (R)   202-225-6205
9 Marcy Kaptur (D)   202-225-4146
10 *Martin Hoke (R)
11 Louis Stokes (D)   202-225-7032
12 John Kasich (R)   202-225-5355
13 *Sherrod Brown (D)
14 Thomas Sawyer (D)   202-225-5231
15 *Deborah Pryce (R)
16 Ralph Regula (R)   202-225-3876
17 James A. Traficant Jr. (D) 202-225-5261
18 Douglas Applegate (D)   202-225-6265

It is always better to contact your congressional representative in his or her home office. You will find that number in your local directory. *New members. Contact U.S. Capitol: 202-224-3121.

185

19 *Eric Fingerhut (D)

Oklahoma
Senate:
David L. Boren (D) 202-224-4721
Don Nickles (R) 202-224-5754

House:
1   James M. Inhofe (R) 202-225-2211
2   Mike Synar (D) 202-225-2701
3   Bill Brewster (D) 202-225-4565
4   Dave McCurdy (D) 202-225-6165
5   *Ernest Jim Istook (R)
6   Glenn English (D) 202-225-5565

Oregon
Senate:
Mark O. Hatfield (R) 202-224-3753
Bob Packwood (R) 202-224-5244

House:
1   *Elizabeth Furse (D)
2   Bob Smith (R) 202-225-6730
3   Ron Wyden (D) 202-225-4811
4   Peter DeFazio (D) 202-225-6416
5   Mike Kopetski (D) 202-225-5711

Pennsylvania
Senate:
Arlen Specter (R) 202-224-4254
Harris Wofford (D) 202-224-6324

House:
1   Thomas Foglietta (D) 202-225-4731
2   Lucien Blackwell (D) 202-225-4001
3   Robert Borski (D) 202-225-8251
4   *Ron Klink (D)
5   Bill Clinger Jr. (R) 202-225-5121
6   *Tim Holden (D)
7   Curt Weldon (R) 202-225-2011
8   *Jim Greenwood (R)
9   Bud Shuster (R) 202-225-2431
10 Joseph McDade (R) 202-225-3731
11 Paul E. Kanjorski (D) 202-225-6511
12 John Murtha (D) 202-225-2065
13 *Marjorie Mezvinsky (D)

It is always better to contact your congressional representative in his or her home office. You will find that number in your local directory. *New members. Contact U.S. Capitol: 202-224-3121.

Congressional Directory

14	William Coyne (D)	202-225-2301
15	*Paul McHale (D)	
16	Robert S. Walker (R)	202-225-2411
17	George Gekas (R)	202-225-4315
18	Rick Santorum (R)	202-225-2135
19	William Goodling (R)	202-225-5836
20	Austin Murphy (D)	202-225-4665
21	Thomas Ridge (R)	202-225-5406

Rhode Island
Senate:
John H. Chafee (R) — 202-224-2921
Claiborne Pell (D) — 202-224-4642

House:
1 Ronald K. Machtley (R) — 202-225-4911
2 Jack Reed (D) — 202-225-2735

South Carolina
Senate:
Ernest F. Hollings (D) — 202-224-6121
Strom Thurmond (R) — 202-224-5972

House
1 Arthur Ravenel Jr. (R) — 202-225-3176
2 Floyd Spence (R) — 202-225-2452
3 Butler Derrick Jr. (D) — 202-225-5301
4 *Bob Inglis (R)
5 John M. Spratt Jr. (D) — 202-225-5501
6 *James Clyburn (D)

South Dakota
Senate:
Tom Daschle (D) — 202-224-2321
Larry Pressler (R) — 202-224-5842

House
At Large, Tim Johnson (D) — 202-225-2801

Tennessee
Senate:
Jim Sasser (D) — 202-224-3344
The Governor of Tennessee will make a temporary appointment to fill Albert Gore's seat.

It is always better to contact your congressional representative in his or her home office. You will find that number in your local directory. *New members. Contact U.S. Capitol: 202-224-3121.

House:
1	Jimmy Quillen (R)	202-225-6356
2	John J. Duncan Jr. (R)	202-225-5435
3	Marilyn Lloyd (D)	202-225-3271
4	Jim Cooper (D)	202-225-6831
5	Bob Clement (D)	202-225-4311
6	Bart Gordon (D)	202-225-4231
7	Don Sundquist (R)	202-225-2811
8	John S. Tanner (D)	202-225-4714
9	Harold E. Ford (D)	202-225-3265

Texas
Senate:
Lloyd Bentsen (D)	202-224-5922
Phil Gramm (R)	202-224-2934

House:
1	Jim Chapman (D)	202-225-3035
2	Charles Wilson (D)	202-225-2401
3	Sam Johnson (R)	202-225-4201
4	Ralph Hall (D)	202-225-6673
5	John Bryant (D)	202-225-2231
6	Joe Barton (R)	202-225-2002
7	Bill Archer (R)	202-225-2571
8	Jack Fields Jr. (R)	202-225-4901
9	Jack Brooks (D)	202-225-6565
10	Jake Pickle (D)	202-225-4865
11	Chet Edwards (D)	202-225-6105
12	Pete Geren (D)	202-225-5071
13	Bill Sarpalius (D)	202-225-3706
14	Greg Laughlin (D)	202-225-2831
15	E. (Kika) de la Garza (D)	202-225-2531
16	Ron Coleman (D)	202-225-4831
17	Charles Stenholm (D)	202-225-6605
18	Craig Washington (D)	202-225-3816
19	Larry Combest (R)	202-225-4005
20	Henry B. Gonzales (D)	202-225-3236
21	Lamar Smith (R)	202-225-4236
22	Tom DeLay (R)	202-225-5951
23	*Henry Bonilla (R)	
24	Martin Frost (D)	202-225-3605
25	Mike A. Andrews (D)	202-225-7508
26	Dick Armey (R)	202-225-7772
27	Solomon Ortiz (D)	202-225-7742
28	*Frank Tejeda (D)	
29	*Gene Green (D)	

It is always better to contact your congressional representative in his or her home office. You will find that number in your local directory. *New members. Contact U.S. Capitol: 202-224-3121.

30 *Eddie Bernice Johnson (D)

Utah
Senate:
*Robert Bennett (R)
Orrin G. Hatch (R)   202-224-5251

House:
1   James V. Hansen (R)   202-225-0453
2   *Karen Shepherd (D)
3   William Orton (D)   202-225-7751

Vermont
Senate:
James Jeffords (R)   202-224-5141
Patrick Leahy (D)   202-224-4242

House:
At Large, Bernie Sanders (O)   202-225-4115

Virginia
Senate:
Charles S. Robb (D)   202-224-4024
John Warner (R)   202-224-2023

House:
1   Herbert H. Bateman (R)   202-225-4261
2   Owen B. Pickett (D)   202-225-4215
3   *Robert Scott (D)
4   Norman Sisisky (D)   202-225-6365
5   Lewis F. Payne Jr. (D)   202-225-4711
6   *Robert Goodlatte (R)
7   Thomas J. Bliley Jr. (R)   202-225-2815
8   James Moran (D)   202-225-4376
9   Rick Boucher (D)   202-225-3861
10 Frank R. Wolf (R)   202-225-5136
11 *Leslie Byrne (D)

Washington
Senate:
Slade Gorton (R)   202-224-3441
*Patty Murray (D)

House:
1   *Maria Cantwell (D)

It is always better to contact your congressional representative in his or her home office. You will find that number in your local directory. *New members. Contact U.S. Capitol: 202-224-3121.

189

2	Al Swift (D)	202-225-2605
3	Jolene Unsoeld (D)	202-225-3536
4	*Jay Inslee (D)	
5	Thomas S. Foley (D)	202-225-2006
6	Norman D. Dicks (D)	202-225-5916
7	Jim McDermott (D)	202-225-3106
8	*Jennifer Dunn (R)	
9	*Mike Kreidler (D)	

West Virginia
Senate:
Robert C. Byrd (D)   202-224-3954
John D. Rockefeller IV (D)   202-224-6472

House:
1   Alan B. Mollohan (D)   202-225-4172
2   Bob Wise Jr. (D)   202-225-2711
3   Nick Joe Rahall II (D)   202-225-3452

Wisconsin
Senate:
*Russell Feingold (D)
Herb Kohl (D)   202-224-5653

House:
1   Les Aspin (D)   202-225-3031
2   Scott Klug (R)   202-225-2906
3   Steve Gunderson (R)   202-225-5506
4   Gerald D. Kleczka (D)   202-225-4572
5   *Thomas Barrett (D)
6   Thomas E. Petri (R)   202-225-2476
7   David R. Obey (D)   202-225-3365
8   Toby Roth (R)   202-225-5665
9   Jim Sensenbrenner (R)   202-225-5101

Wyoming
Senate:
Alan K. Simpson (R)   202-224-3424
Malcolm Wallop (R)   202-224-6441

House
At Large, Craig Thomas (R)   202-225-2311

It is always better to contact your congressional representative in his or her home office. You will find that number in your local directory. *New members. Contact U.S. Capitol: 202-224-3121.

NFIB Membership Enrollment Form

*Join the fight for small business!
Join NFIB today.*

Suite 700
600 Maryland Avenue, SW
Washington, D.C. 20024

For information about joining NFIB, photocopy this page, complete the form below and mail it to the above address. Or you may call 1-800-274-NFIB.

Name_____
     First Name   Middle Initial   Last Name

Firm Name_____

Business Address_____

City_____State_____ZIP_____

Business Phone (   )_____ No. of Employees_____

Type of Business_____